180°   150°   120°   90°   60°   30°

ARCTIC OCEAN

Queen Elizabeth Islands

Ellesmere Island

Greenland

East Siberian Sea

Chukchi Sea

Beaufort Sea

Banks Island

Victoria Island

Baffin Bay

Baffin Island

Davis Strait

Brooks Range

Kolyma Range

Yukon

Mackenzie

Mackenzie Mountains

Great Bear Lake

Mount McKinley (Denali) 20,322 ft

Alaska Range

Great Slave Lake

Hudson Bay

Labrador Sea

Kamchatka Peninsula

Bering Sea

Gulf of Alaska

Coast Mountains

NORTH AMERICA

Canadian Shield

Aleutian Islands

Queen Charlotte Islands

Vancouver Island

Rocky Mountains

Lake Winnipeg

Newfoundland

PACIFIC OCEAN

Great Basin

Great Plains

Missouri

Great Lakes

Nova Scotia

ATLANTIC OCEAN

Colorado

Ohio

Appalachian Mts.

Mississippi

Midway Islands

Hawaiian Islands

Rio Grande

Sierra Madre Oriental

Gulf of Mexico

Bermuda

Hawaii

Sierra Madre Occidental

Bahamas

Marshall Islands

Cuba

Greater Antilles

West Indies

Tropic o

ronesia

Tungaru

Line Islands

Melanesia

Polynesia

Caribbean Sea

Lesser Antilles

Llanos

Orinoco

Guiana Highlands

Solomon Islands

Galapagos Islands

Amazon

Samoa

Marquesas Islands

Amazon Basin

Vanuatu

Cook Islands

PACIFIC OCEAN

Amazon

SOUTH AMERICA

Fiji

Tuamotu Islands

Andes

New Caledonia

Tonga

Brazilian Highlands

Pitcairn Islands

Gran Chaco

Tropic o

Austral Islands

Paraguay

Easter Island

Juan Fernandez Islands

Paraná

Uruguay

Tasman Sea

North Island

Cerro Aconcagua 22,831 ft

Pampas

South Island

Chatham Islands

New Zealand

Patagonia

ATLANTIC OCEAN

Falkland Islands

Tierra del Fuego

Cape Horn

South Georgia

South Sandwich Islands

SOUTHERN OCEAN

Antarctic Peninsula

Ant

180°   150°   120°   90°   60°   30°

World
Atlas

Sandy Creek
NEW YORK

An Imprint of Sterling Publishing
387 Park Avenue South
New York, NY 10016

SANDY CREEK and the distinctive Sandy Creek logo
are registered trademarks of Barnes & Noble, Inc.

Originally created by Picthall & Gunzi Ltd ©2008
This edition copyright Award Publications Limited ©2013

This edition published by Sandy Creek.

Digital Cartography: Encompass Graphics Ltd
Cartographic Consultant: Roger Bullen
Editorial Direction: Christiane Gunzi
Senior Editor: Louise Pritchard
Art Direction: Chez Picthall
Design: Gillian Shaw and Paul Calver
Map Indexing: Roger Bullen and Paula Metcalf
General Indexer: Angie Hipkin
Original text: Chez Picthall & Christiane Gunzi

All rights reserved. No part of this publication
may be reproduced, stored in a retrieval
system or transmitted in any form or by any
means, electronic, mechanical, photocopying,
recording or otherwise, without the prior
written permission of the publisher.

ISBN 978-1-4351-4828-4

Reproduction by Colourscan, Singapore
Manufactured by KHL Printing Co. Pte Ltd, Singapore
Printed and bound in Singapore
Lot #: 2 4 6 8 10 9 7 5 3 1
04/13

World Atlas

Chez Picthall

Sandy Creek
NEW YORK

Contents

South America

Africa

North America

Europe

Asia

Australasia and Oceania

The Arctic and Antarctica

All about maps

Maps show us what places on Earth look like from above. They give useful information, such as where towns and cities are, or where rivers and mountains run. A map can help us to find out where we are and can show us the distances between places. Maps have to carry a lot of information, so different symbols, lines, and colors are used to show the features on the Earth's surface. Symbols are often used to show the position of towns, and lines show where all the country borders and rivers are.

A street map

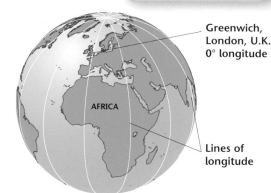
A country map

Map scales Maps are "large-" or "small-" scale. Large-scale maps show small areas with lots of detail, like the street map above. Small-scale maps show large areas with less detail, like this country map. All the maps in this atlas are small-scale.

How maps are made

The most accurate world maps are globes because they are the same shape as planet Earth. To make a flat map out of a globe, map makers have to change the shape of Earth's surface. The land shapes get stretched and distorted. Map makers do this work mathematically, using what is called a "projection." There are many different kinds of projection, and each one looks slightly different. The people who create maps are called "cartographers."

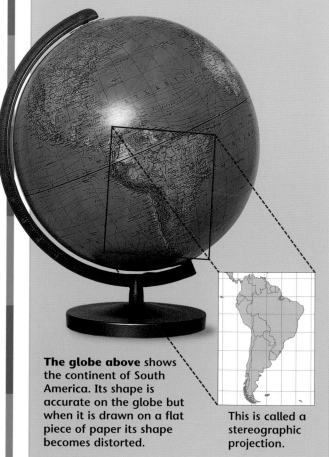

The globe above shows the continent of South America. Its shape is accurate on the globe but when it is drawn on a flat piece of paper its shape becomes distorted.

This is called a stereographic projection.

Latitude and longitude lines

To help us to locate places, we have invented invisible lines that run around the Earth. These are called the lines of latitude and longitude. Lines of latitude run horizontally. They measure how far north or south a place is from the Equator (around the Earth's middle). Longitude lines run from the North to the South Pole and measure how far east or west a place is from Greenwich, London, England. All these measurements are in degrees and show a place's position on Earth.

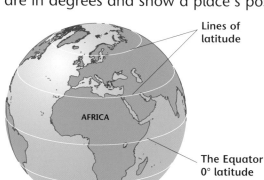

Lines of latitude

AFRICA

The Equator 0° latitude

Greenwich, London, U.K. 0° longitude

AFRICA

Lines of longitude

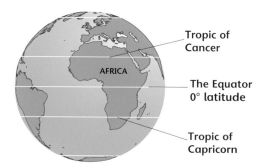

Tropic of Cancer

AFRICA

The Equator 0° latitude

Tropic of Capricorn

The Equator and the Tropics

The Equator is an imaginary line that runs around the center of the Earth. It is an equal distance from the North and South Poles. Lying parallel to the Equator are lines called the Tropics of Cancer and Capricorn. Between these lines the climate and land are tropical.

North and South Poles

The North and South Poles are the most northerly and southerly points on the surface of the Earth. They are invisible and are found where all the lines of longitude meet. If you stood on the South Pole every direction would be north, and at the North Pole all directions would be south! There is no land at the North Pole, just the frozen waters of the Arctic Ocean.

North Pole

AFRICA

AFRICA

South Pole

How to use this atlas

The maps in this atlas have been arranged by continent in the following order: North America, South America, Africa, Europe, Asia, Australasia, Oceania, and Antarctica. Every map has a double page and the countries on each map are listed at the top left-hand side for easy reference. Antarctica is shown with the Arctic, after all the other maps. Every map is accompanied by photographs of landscapes, wildlife, industries, famous landmarks, typical foods, and interesting facts, to give you a snapshot of each area.

The indexes

This atlas has two indexes. One index gives a list of all the place names shown on the maps. The other index lists the animals, industries, and other topics in the book. To find out how to use the indexes, see p.60.

Index to place names

Regional heading tells you which region or country the map shows.

Continent heading tells you which continent the region is in.

Introductory text sets the scene for each map, giving general information about the region.

Did you know? boxes give you some fascinating facts about the countries on each of the maps.

Locator globe shows you which region of the world the map covers.

Country File lists all the countries shown on the map.

Photographs of animals, people, and places help to bring the map to life.

Compass rose shows the direction of north for each map.

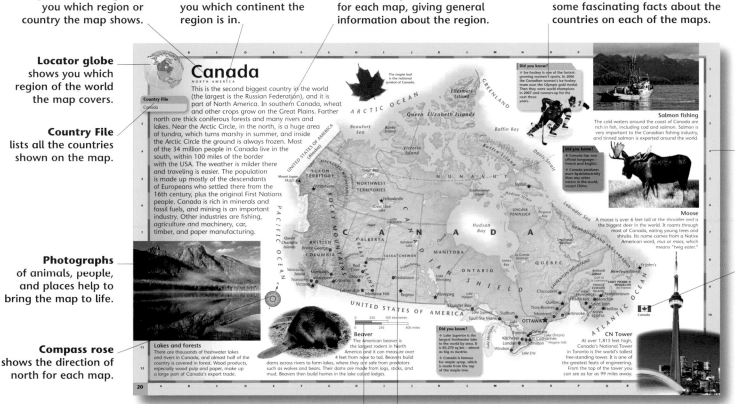

Grid letters and numbers help you to find the cities, towns, rivers, mountains, and other features listed in the index to the place names.

Flags of each nation are shown next to their country.

Scale bar helps you to work out the distances between places and how big countries are.

Map colors show you how high the land is.

Key to all the features on the maps:

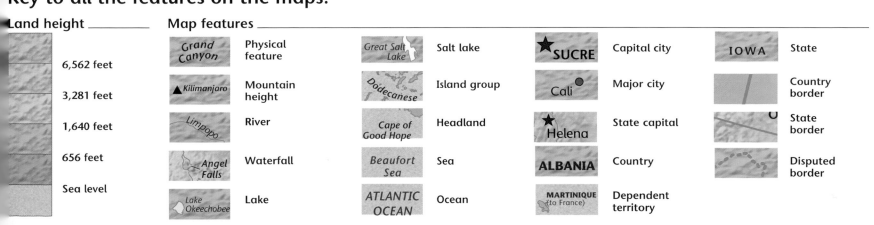

Land height

6,562 feet
3,281 feet
1,640 feet
656 feet
Sea level

Map features

Grand Canyon	Physical feature	Great Salt Lake	Salt lake	★ SUCRE	Capital city
▲ Kilimanjaro	Mountain height	Dodecanese	Island group	Cali ●	Major city
Limpopo	River	Cape of Good Hope	Headland	★ Helena	State capital
Angel Falls	Waterfall	Beaufort Sea	Sea	ALBANIA	Country
Lake Okeechobee	Lake	ATLANTIC OCEAN	Ocean	MARTINIQUE (to France)	Dependent territory

IOWA	State
	Country border
	State border
	Disputed border

Our planet in space

If we wrote down the address for planet Earth it would be: The Earth, The Solar System, The Milky Way, The Universe. Our Earth belongs to the Solar System, which forms just a tiny part of the Milky Way galaxy. A galaxy is a massive group of hundreds of billions of stars. The Milky Way is one of billions of galaxies in the Universe. The Universe is the name that we give to the whole of space.

The Milky Way

Our Sun is one of 200 billion stars in the Milky Way. The Milky Way is a spiral galaxy and it is really enormous. It would take 100,000 "light years" to travel across it!

The Solar System

Our Solar System is made up of the Sun and the eight planets and other bodies (such as comets, moons, and asteroids) that orbit around it. The Sun is a star. Its powerful gravity keeps everything orbiting around it. The four planets that are nearest to the Sun (Mercury, Venus, Earth, and Mars) are made of rock and metal. The four outer planets (Jupiter, Saturn, Uranus, and Neptune) are mostly gas or liquid. They are known as "the gas giants."

Saturn

This planet is surrounded by many "rings." These rings are hundreds of feet thick and about 170,000 miles in diameter. They are formed from millions of icy particles. The ice particles range in size from tiny pieces a quarter of an inch across to huge lumps that are over 30 feet across.

Did you know?

◈ Distances in space are so huge that scientists measure them in "light years." A light year is the distance that light travels in one year, which is around 5,878 billion miles!

◈ The light coming from the Sun takes a little over eight minutes to reach Earth.

Pluto

Pluto used to be called a planet. But in 2006 the International Astronomical Union decided that it is only a "dwarf planet."

Neptune

This is the farthest planet from the Sun. A French mathematician discovered its existence in 1843 by doing calculations, but it was not actually seen for another three years.

Uranus

The blue color of Uranus comes from the gas called methane, which is in its atmosphere. Scientists think that this planet is made of different icy materials (methane, water, and ammonia) surrounding a solid core.

The relative distance of the planets from the Sun

Sun

Venus

Neptune
This is about 2.8 billion miles from the Sun.

Uranus

Saturn

Jupiter

Earth

Mars

Mercury

The Sun

The Sun is about 4.5 billion years old and is only half-way through its life. It is 870,000 miles across and is made mostly of the gases hydrogen and helium. The temperature at its surface is 9,921°F.

The Moon
Earth's Moon has no water and is made of solid rock. It is covered in craters made by meteorites that crashed into it.

Earth
The Earth is the third planet from the Sun and, as far as we know, it is the only planet in our Solar System that has any kind of life on it.

Venus
The planet Venus is the brightest object in our night sky, after the Moon. This is because its atmosphere reflects more sunlight than any other planet.

Mercury
The planet that is closest to the Sun is Mercury. This means that it has the shortest year (the time that it takes to go once round the Sun) of all the planets.

Mars

Bright red dust covers most of the planet Mars. The dust often blows into fierce sandstorms. When this happens, the surface of the planet cannot be seen.

Jupiter
This giant planet is made almost entirely of gas. Jupiter is the largest planet in the Solar System and it is 11 times larger in diameter than Earth.

Did you know?

To qualify as a planet, a body must:
1) Orbit around a sun.
2) Be big enough for its own gravity to have pulled it into a ball.
3) Have cleared other bodies out of its orbit.

Pluto does not qualify on the third point, so in 2006 it was downgraded from a planet to a "dwarf planet."

Planet Earth's many layers

The rocky layer of Earth that we live on is called the crust. It is around 25 miles thick. Scientists believe that the inner core of Earth is solid iron. This is surrounded by a molten layer of iron and nickel, which is called the outer core. Between the Earth's outer core and its crust is the mantle.

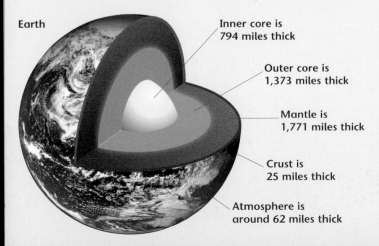

Earth

Inner core is 794 miles thick

Outer core is 1,373 miles thick

Mantle is 1,771 miles thick

Crust is 25 miles thick

Atmosphere is around 62 miles thick

When the surface of the Earth moves

The Earth's crust is made up of "tectonic plates," which are constantly moving and pushing past each other. Most of the time the movements are so small that we do not notice them. But sometimes, during an earthquake or a volcanic eruption, the Earth moves violently and these movements are easy to notice.

Earthquake
When tectonic plates "stick" together instead of sliding past each other, stress builds up in the rocks until they crack or "fault." This cracking sends shock waves through the Earth, causing an earthquake. Powerful earthquakes can sometimes destroy whole cities.

Volcano
Where the Earth's crust is weak, or at the point between two tectonic plates, magma (molten rock) seeps out and volcanoes can develop over time. The pressure of magma pushing up to the Earth's surface can be so powerful that a volcano will erupt, spewing out lava.

Physical features of the world

30° 0° 30° 60° 90° 120°

Greenland

Greenland Sea

Spitsbergen

Franz Josef Land

Severnaya Zemlya

Novaya Zemlya

Kara Sea

Taymyr Peninsula

Laptev Sea

New Siberi Islands

Arctic Circle

Denmark Strait

Iceland

Faeroe Islands

Norwegian Sea

Barents Sea

North Siberian Lowland

Central Siberian Plateau

Pechora

Northern Dvina

Ob'

West Siberian Plain

S i b e r i a

Lena

Verkhoyanskiy Khrebet

60°

Scandinavia

Lake Ladoga

Lake Onega

Yenisey

Ob'

Angara

Lena

Aldan

Se Okl

North Sea

Ireland

Britain

Baltic Sea

North European Plain

Volga

U r a l   M o u n t a i n s

Yenisey

Irtysh

Lake Baikal

Amur

Sakh

EUROPE

Rhine

Carpathian Mountains

Dnieper

A S I A

ATLANTIC

Alps

Loire

Don

Volga

Lake Balkhash

Altai Mountains

Manchurian Plain

Bay of Biscay

Danube

Black Sea

Caspian Sea

Aral Sea

Tien Shan

Gobi

OCEAN

Caucasus
El'brus
18,510 ft

Sea of Japan

Hok

Iberian Peninsula

Azores

Anatolia

Mediterranean Sea

Zagros Mountains

Iranian Plateau

Hindu Kush

Takla Makan Desert

H i m a l a y a s

Yellow River

Great Plain of China

Yellow Sea

Honsh

Atlas Mountains

Tigris

Euphrates

The Gulf

Plateau of Tibet

Brahmaputra

Shikoku
Kyushu

30°

Canary Islands

Libyan Desert

Indus

Thar Desert

Ganges

Mount Everest
29,035 ft

Yangtze

Xi Jiang

East China Sea

Tropic of Cancer

S a h a r a   D e s e r t

Nile

Red Sea

Arabian Peninsula

Arabian Sea

Deccan

Bay of Bengal

Salween

Mekong

Irrawaddy

Taiwan

Philippine Sea

Mariana Islands

Cape Verde Islands

Senegal

Niger

S a h e l

Lake Chad

White Nile

Blue Nile

Gulf of Aden

Laccadive Islands

Andaman Islands

South China Sea

Phillipine Islands

M

AFRICA

Ethiopian Highlands

Maldive Islands

Nicobar Islands

Sri Lanka

Malay Peninsula

Celebes Sea

Ca Is

Equator

Gulf of Guinea

Ubangi

Congo

Congo Basin

Great Rift Valley

Great Rift Valley

Lake Victoria

Kilimanjaro
19,341 ft

Seychelles

Chagos Archipelago

Sumatra

Borneo

Java Sea

Sulawesi

East Indies

New Guinea

Ascension Island

Lake Tanganyika

Java

Timor

Arafura Sea

St Helena

Zambezi

Lake Nyasa

Comoros Islands

Madagascar

Mozambique Channel

Mauritius

Réunion

Cocos Islands

INDIAN

Tropic of Capricorn

Namib Desert

Kalahari Desert

OCEAN

Great Sandy Desert

Simpson Desert

Great

ATLANTIC

Orange River

AUSTRALIA

30°

OCEAN

Cape of Good Hope

Nullarbor Plain

Great Australian Bight

Moun Kosciuszk
7,310

Prince Edward Islands

Crozet Islands

Tasmania

Kerguelen

60°

S O U T H E R N   O C E A N

Antarctic Circle

A N T A R C T I C A

30° 0° 30° 60° 90° 120°

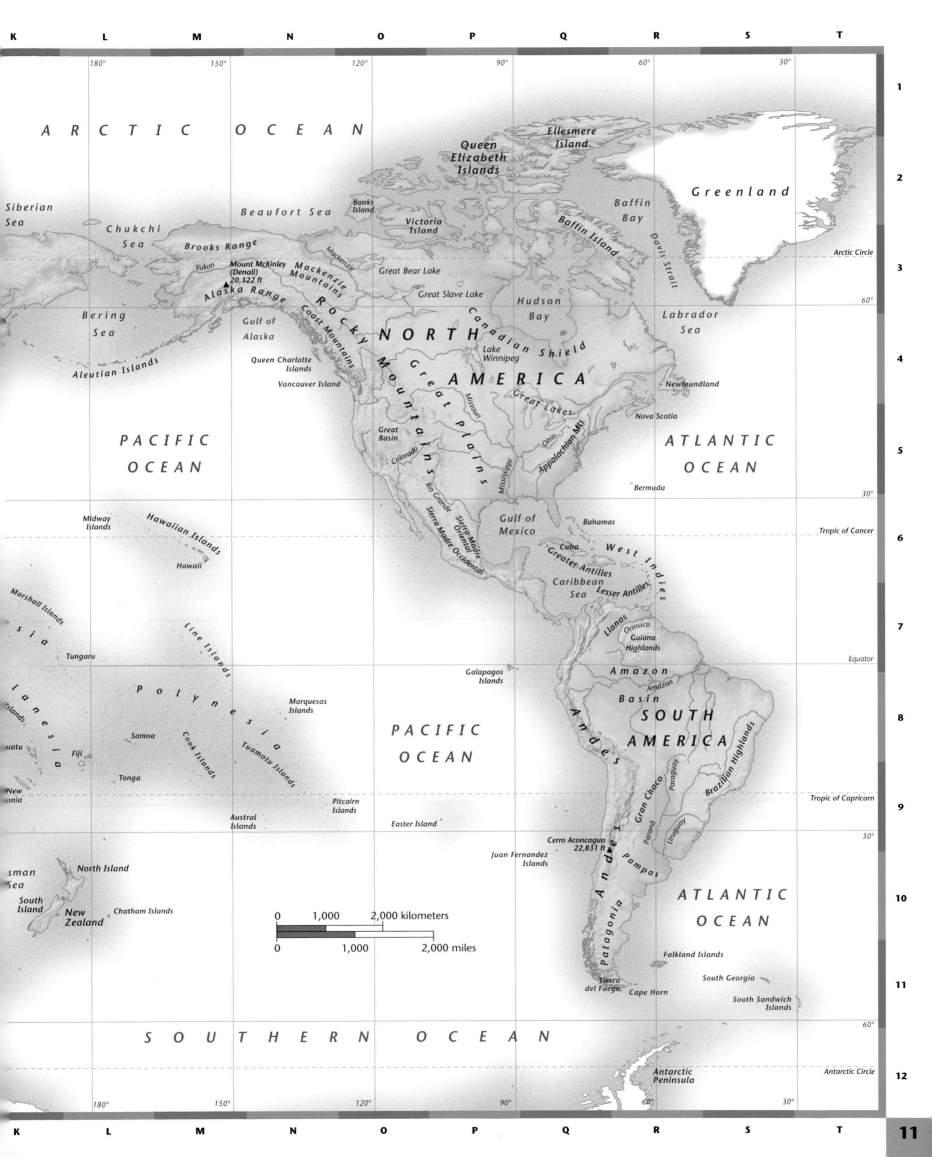

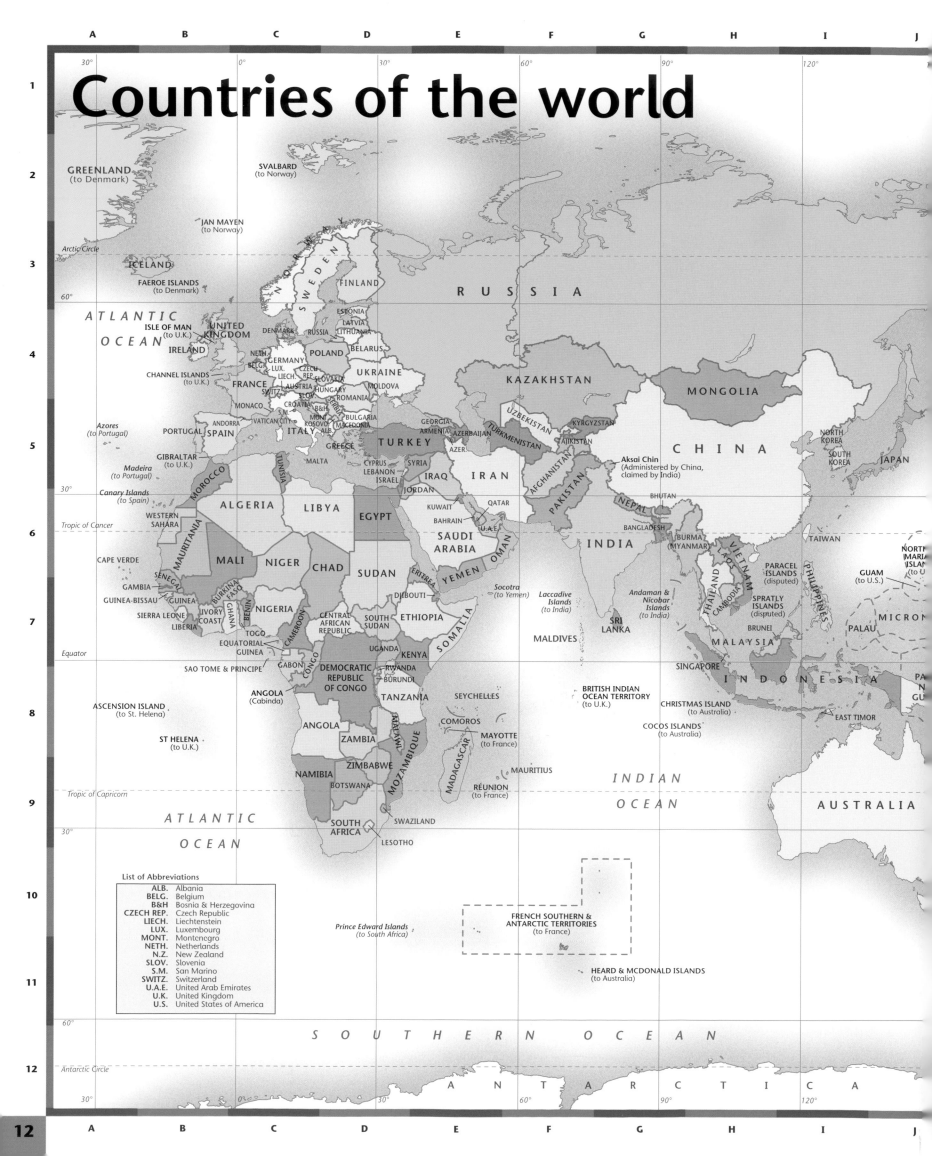

Countries of the world

List of Abbreviations

ALB.	Albania
BELG.	Belgium
B&H	Bosnia & Herzegovina
CZECH REP.	Czech Republic
LIECH.	Liechtenstein
LUX.	Luxembourg
MONT.	Montenegro
NETH.	Netherlands
N.Z.	New Zealand
SLOV.	Slovenia
S.M.	San Marino
SWITZ.	Switzerland
U.A.E.	United Arab Emirates
U.K.	United Kingdom
U.S.	United States of America

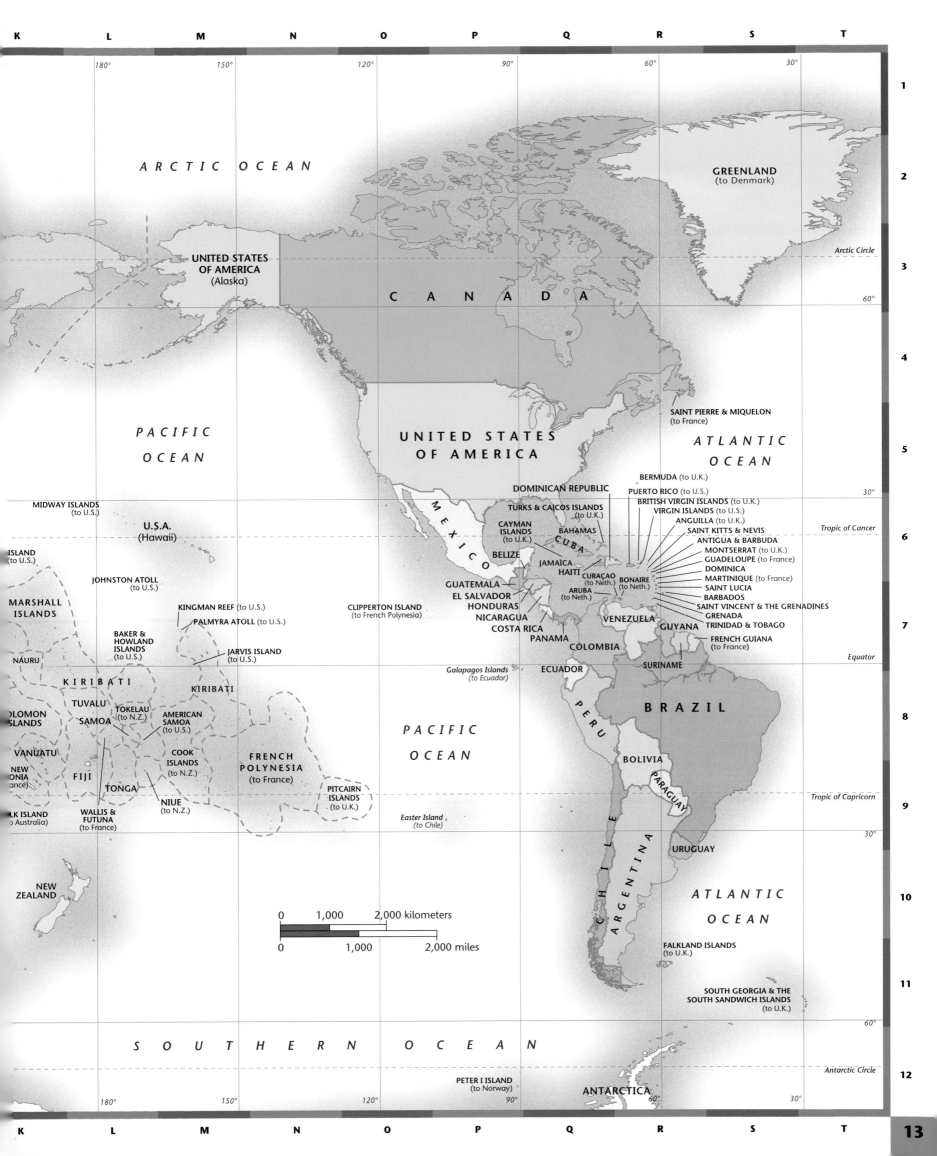

180°   150°   120°   90°   60°   30°

1

ARCTIC OCEAN

GREENLAND
(to Denmark)

2

Arctic Circle

UNITED STATES
OF AMERICA
(Alaska)

3

C A N A D A

60°

4

PACIFIC
OCEAN

SAINT PIERRE & MIQUELON
(to France)

ATLANTIC
OCEAN

5

UNITED STATES
OF AMERICA

BERMUDA (to U.K.)

DOMINICAN REPUBLIC

30°

PUERTO RICO (to U.S.)

MIDWAY ISLANDS
(to U.S.)

TURKS & CAICOS ISLANDS
(to U.K.)

BRITISH VIRGIN ISLANDS (to U.K.)
VIRGIN ISLANDS (to U.S.)

Tropic of Cancer

U.S.A.
(Hawaii)

MEXICO

CAYMAN
ISLANDS
(to U.K.)

BAHAMAS

ANGUILLA (to U.K.)
SAINT KITTS & NEVIS
ANTIGUA & BARBUDA

ISLAND
(to U.S.)

CUBA

MONTSERRAT (to U.K.)
GUADELOUPE (to France)

JOHNSTON ATOLL
(to U.S.)

BELIZE

JAMAICA

DOMINICA

HAITI

MARTINIQUE (to France)

MARSHALL
ISLANDS

KINGMAN REEF (to U.S.)

GUATEMALA

CURAÇAO
(to Neth.)

BONAIRE
(to Neth.)

SAINT LUCIA

PALMYRA ATOLL (to U.S.)

EL SALVADOR

ARUBA
(to Neth.)

BARBADOS
SAINT VINCENT & THE GRENADINES

HONDURAS

GRENADA

BAKER &
HOWLAND
ISLANDS
(to U.S.)

JARVIS ISLAND
(to U.S.)

CLIPPERTON ISLAND
(to French Polynesia)

NICARAGUA

VENEZUELA

TRINIDAD & TOBAGO

GUYANA

NAURU

COSTA RICA
PANAMA

FRENCH GUIANA
(to France)

7

COLOMBIA

SURINAME

Equator

KIRIBATI

KIRIBATI

Galapagos Islands
(to Ecuador)

ECUADOR

OLOMON
SLANDS

TUVALU

PERU

B R A Z I L

8

SAMOA

TOKELAU
(to N.Z.)

AMERICAN
SAMOA
(to U.S.)

VANUATU

COOK
ISLANDS
(to N.Z.)

FRENCH
POLYNESIA
(to France)

BOLIVIA

NEW
ONIA
ance)

FIJI

PARAGUAY

TONGA

PITCAIRN
ISLANDS
(to U.K.)

Tropic of Capricorn

K ISLAND
Australia)

WALLIS &
FUTUNA
(to France)

NIUE
(to N.Z.)

Easter Island
(to Chile)

CHILE

ARGENTINA

URUGUAY

30°

NEW
ZEALAND

PACIFIC
OCEAN

SOUTHERN OCEAN

ATLANTIC
OCEAN

10

0   1,000   2,000 kilometers

0   1,000   2,000 miles

FALKLAND ISLANDS
(to U.K.)

11

SOUTH GEORGIA & THE
SOUTH SANDWICH ISLANDS
(to U.K.)

60°

12

Antarctic Circle

PETER I ISLAND
(to Norway)

ANTARCTICA

180°   150°   120°   90°   60°   30°

Climate and land cover

Climate is the average pattern of the weather over around 30 years. The climate of a place depends on how much sunshine and rain it gets, how close it is to the sea and sea currents, and how high it is above sea level. Different kinds of plants grow in different climates. The type of vegetation in an area, such as grassland or tropical forest, is called "land cover." Different land cover is suitable for different animals. The countries around the Equator get the most sunlight and rain. It is there that the habitats with the largest numbers of animals and plants are found. In places where there is little rainfall or the temperatures are too hot or cold, such as the Sahara or the North and South Poles, only a few species of plants and animals are able to survive.

Temperate broadleaf forest
Forests in temperate parts of the world have mild temperatures and plenty of rain. These forests contain trees such as oak, beech, birch, and chestnut. Broadleaved trees collect nutrients in summer and shed their leaves in the fall to save energy and water.

Tropical broadleaf forest
Tropical forests that grow near the Equator have high temperatures and receive heavy rainfall all year round. These forests may contain over 50,000 different species of trees, as well as huge numbers of other plants and animals.

Earth's changing climate
The world's climate is gradually changing, and this is having huge effects on its wildlife and people. Some areas have unusual floods and other places are affected by drought. Many kinds of animals, including polar bears, are threatened by climate change. Not all the animals and plants will be able to adapt to these new conditions. In the most badly affected areas some species will die out.

Did you know?

◈ The Sun's rays are stronger at the Equator than at the North and South Poles. This is why the weather is hot in tropical regions and cold in polar regions.

◈ The different environments (habitats) on planet Earth where life exists are called biomes. A certain area, such as a forest or desert, is called an ecosystem.

Extreme weather
Violent storms, heavy rainfall, strong winds, and long periods of sunshine are all examples of extreme weather. Extreme weather often causes widespread flooding or drought, and the effects of these can be devastating. People may be killed or left homeless, and crops, farm animals, and wildlife may be destroyed.

■ Needleleaf forest

Stretching across northern parts of Asia, Europe, and North America is a belt of tall, evergreen trees with needle-like leaves. They can survive cold winters because they gather nutrients all year.

■ Cropland

Many of the most fertile areas of the world, especially Europe and North America, do not have their natural land cover. This has been cleared over hundreds of years to grow crops for food.

■ Grassland

In areas of a continent where there is not enough rain for trees to grow, there are huge grasslands. These are called steppes and prairies in the north. In South America they are known as pampas.

■ Tundra

Areas of tundra are mostly found near the Arctic Circle. The soil is frozen for much of the year. In places where it melts for a few months, plants such as lichens, mosses, and low shrubs are able to grow.

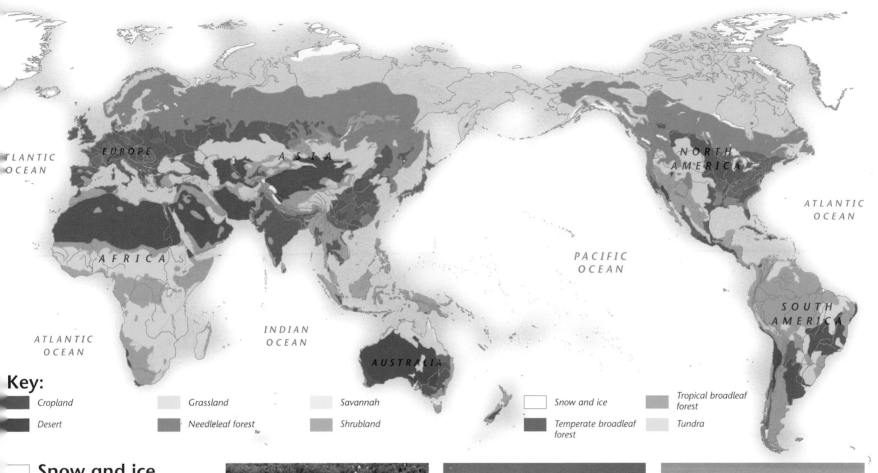

Key:

- ■ Cropland
- ■ Desert
- ■ Grassland
- ■ Needleleaf forest
- Savannah
- ■ Shrubland
- □ Snow and ice
- ■ Temperate broadleaf forest
- ■ Tropical broadleaf forest
- Tundra

☐ Snow and ice

In the Arctic and Antarctica, and on the highest parts of mountain ranges, such as the Alps and the Andes, there is snow and ice all year round. Temperatures remain well below freezing and it is often windy. Very few animals and plants can survive in such a harsh environment.

■ Shrubland

At the edges of both hot and cold deserts there are areas of shrubland. Where it is too hot or too cold for trees to survive, tough, spiny shrubs with small leaves grow well.

■ Desert

Deserts have very little water and are often windy. Few plants or animals can survive, as temperatures soar to over 104°F in the day and drop to below freezing at night.

■ Savannah

Between hot deserts and tropical forests are areas called savannah. There is grass here and lots of trees, but the trees do not grow close together in big groups.

Planet Earth's population

About 100 years ago, there were 1,625 million people on Earth, but in 2012 the world's population reached seven billion people. Every second, our planet's population gets larger by two or three people. If this rate of growth continues there could be another billion people living on Earth in 12 to 13 years' time. People live in most parts of the world, but they are not evenly distributed. Some countries, such as Singapore, have dense populations with thousands of people for every square mile of land (which is called its population density), but others, such as Mongolia, have fewer than six people for every square mile. Most of the areas where hardly any people live are either too hot and dry, such as the Sahara, or too cold, such as the poles.

Is there enough for everyone?
As the world's population continues to grow bigger, more houses, food, water, and fuel are needed. In some areas there is not enough clean water or shelter for everyone. Some countries cannot grow enough food, and do not have enough fuel supplies.

World population
This map shows how the world's population is spread out. Most people live in South and East Asia. In 1900 only a few towns had more than 1 million people living in them. Now 25 of the world's cities have over 15 million people.

EUROPE has mostly warm summers and mild winters, and much of the land is fertile and easy to farm, which provides ideal living conditions.

AFRICA has the Sahara, which is the biggest desert in the world. Living here is difficult because the temperatures range from 122°F during the day to below 32°F at night. Most people living here belong to nomadic tribes.

ATLANTIC OCEAN

RUSSIAN FEDERATION

ASIA

Cairo

Karachi

Delhi

Seoul
Tokyo
Osaka
Shanghai

Mumbai

Kolkata

Manila

AFRICA

SOUTH ASIA has the biggest, and one of the fastest-growing populations in the world. One-fifth of the world's population lives in this area.

Jakarta

AUSTRALIA

INDIAN OCEAN

Busy, busy cities
In the 1900s, only 1 out of every 10 people lived in a city. Now more than 5 out of 10 people live in cities. India and China have the most cities with over one million people, even though two-thirds of their populations live in the countryside. By 2030 almost two-thirds of the world's population may live in cities.

Population growth

The world's population is now more than six times bigger than it was 200 years ago. This is mostly due to better healthcare and improved ways of growing food and supplying clean water. A well-fed population with better healthcare means that more babies are being born alive and more of them survive, and people are living longer too.

These are the most populated countries in the world.

In 2012 there were 11 countries with national populations of more than 100,000,000 people.

1	China	1,336,718,015
2	India	1,189,172,906
3	USA	313,232,044
4	Indonesia	245,613,043
5	Brazil	203,429,773
6	Pakistan	187,342,721
9	Bangladesh	158,570,535
7	Nigeria	155,215,573
8	Russia	138,739,892
10	Japan	126,475,664
11	Mexico	113,724,226

Controlling the population

In some parts of the world people have large families. This can be because of religious beliefs, traditions, or due to poverty. To help slow down population growth, many governments now teach people how to plan their families better. In China the government has ruled that couples may not have more than one child without permission.

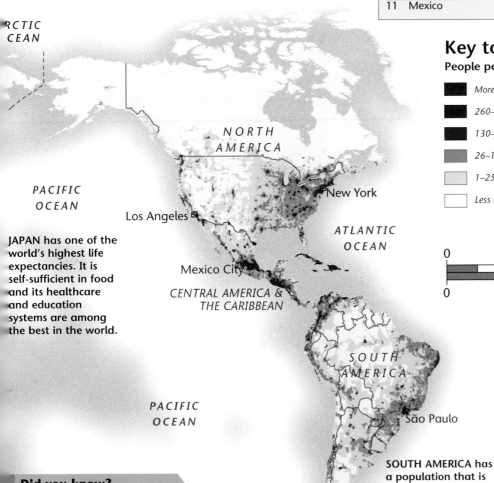

JAPAN has one of the world's highest life expectancies. It is self-sufficient in food and its healthcare and education systems are among the best in the world.

Key to the map:
People per square mile

- More than 2,600
- 260–2,599
- 130–259
- 26–129
- 1–25
- Less than 1

0   2,000 kilometers

0   2,000 miles

SOUTH AMERICA has a population that is mainly around the coast and in the northern parts of the Andes. The population in many towns has grown enormously because people have moved from the countryside to the towns to find work.

How long people live

The number of years that people are likely to live is called their "life expectancy." People in different countries have different life expectancies. In countries where there is not enough food or clean water, people are not expected to live to an old age. Swaziland has a high amount of the HIV/AIDS disease, and life expectancy is 32 years. Japan is one of the richest countries and has one of the highest life expectancies, at about 82 years. The country with the highest is Andorra, at over 83 years.

Flags and facts

All the countries in the world have their own national flag. Each flag is a colorful symbol of its country's people and government. The population of every country changes daily. Most countries have growing populations, although some decrease due to war, natural disasters, or political pressure. Below is a list of all the continents and countries. Each country's flag, capital city, and population are included.

NORTH AMERICA
Canada p.20

Canada
Capital City Ottawa
Population 34,030,589

USA p.22

United States of America
Capital City Washington D.C.
Population 313,232,044

Central America and the Caribbean p.24

Antigua and Barbuda
Capital City St. John's
Population 87,884

Bahamas
Capital City Nassau
Population 313,312

Barbados
Capital City Bridgetown
Population 286,705

Belize
Capital City Belmopan
Population 321,115

Costa Rica
Capital City San Jose
Population 4,576,562

Cuba
Capital City Havana
Population 11,087,330

Dominica
Capital City Roseau
Population 72,969

Dominican Republic
Capital City Santo Domingo
Population 9,956,648

El Salvador
Capital City San Salvador
Population 6,071,774

Grenada
Capital City St. George's
Population 108,419

Guatemala
Capital City Guatemala City
Population 13,824,463

Haiti
Capital City Port-au-Prince
Population 9,719,932

Honduras
Capital City Tegucigalpa
Population 8,143,564

Jamaica
Capital City Kingston
Population 2,868,380

Mexico
Capital City Mexico City
Population 113,724,226

Nicaragua
Capital City Managua
Population 5,666,301

Panama
Capital City Panama City
Population 3,460,462

St. Lucia
Capital City Castries
Population 161,557

St. Kitts and Nevis
Capital City Basseterre
Population 50,314

St. Vincent and the Grenadines
Capital City Kingstown
Population 103,869

Trinidad and Tobago
Capital City Port-of-Spain
Population 1,227,505

SOUTH AMERICA
South America p.26

Argentina
Capital City Buenos Aires
Population 41,769,726

Bolivia
Capital Cities La Paz and Sucre
Population 10,118,683

Brazil
Capital City Brasilia
Population 203,429,773

Chile
Capital City Santiago
Population 16,888,760

Colombia
Capital City Bogota
Population 44,725,543

Ecuador
Capital City Quito
Population 15,007,343

Guyana
Capital City Georgetown
Population 744,768

Paraguay
Capital City Asuncion
Population 6,459,058

Peru
Capital City Lima
Population 29,248,943

Suriname
Capital City Paramaribo
Population 491,989

Uruguay
Capital City Montevideo
Population 3,308,535

Venezuela
Capital City Caracas
Population 27,635,743

AFRICA
Northern Africa p.28

Algeria
Capital City Algiers
Population 34,994,937

Benin
Capital City Porto-Novo
Population 9,325,032

Burkina Faso
Capital City Ouagadougou
Population 16,751,455

Cameroon
Capital City Yaounde
Population 19,711,291

Cape Verde
Capital City Praia
Population 516,100

Central African Republic
Capital City Bangui
Population 4,950,027

Chad
Capital City Ndjamena
Population 10,758,945

Djibouti
Capital City Djibouti
Population 757,074

Egypt
Capital City Cairo
Population 82,079,636

Eritrea
Capital City Asmara
Population 5,939,484

Ethiopia
Capital City Addis Ababa
Population 90,873,739

Gambia
Capital City Banjul
Population 1,797,860

Ghana
Capital City Accra
Population 24,791,073

Guinea
Capital City Conakry
Population 10,601,009

Guinea-Bissau
Capital City Bissau
Population 1,596,677

Ivory Coast
Capital City Yamoussoukro
Population 21,504,162

Liberia
Capital City Monrovia
Population 3,786,764

Libya
Capital City Tripoli
Population 6,597,960

Mali
Capital City Bamako
Population 14,159,904

Mauritania
Capital City Nouakchott
Population 3,281,634

Morocco
Capital City Rabat
Population 31,968,361

Niger
Capital City Niamey
Population 16,468,886

Nigeria
Capital City Abuja
Population 155,215,573

Senegal
Capital City Dakar
Population 12,643,799

Sierra Leone
Capital City Freetown
Population 5,363,669

Somalia
Capital City Mogadishu
Population 9,925,640

South Sudan
Capital City Juba
Population 8,260,490

Sudan
Capital City Khartoum
Population 45,047,502

Togo
Capital City Lome
Population 6,771,993

Tunisia
Capital City Tunis
Population 10,629,186

Western Sahara
Capital City Laayoune
Population 507,160

Southern Africa p.30

Angola
Capital City Luanda
Population 13,338,541

Botswana
Capital City Gaborone
Population 2,065,398

Burundi
Capital City Bujumbura
Population 10,216,190

Comoros
Capital City Moroni
Population 794,683

Congo
Capital City Brazzaville
Population 4,243,929

Congo, DR
Capital City Kinshasa
Population 71,712,867

Equatorial Guinea
Capital City Malabo
Population 668,225

Gabon
Capital City Libreville
Population 1,576,665

Kenya
Capital City Nairobi
Population 41,070,934

Lesotho
Capital City Maseru
Population 1,924,886

Madagascar
Capital City Antananarivo
Population 21,926,221

Malawi
Capital City Lilongwe
Population 15,879,252

Mauritius
Capital City Port Louis
Population 1,303,717

Mozambique
Capital City Maputo
Population 22,948,858

Namibia
Capital City Windhoek
Population 2,147,585

Rwanda
Capital City Kigali
Population 11,370,425

São Tome and Principe
Capital City Sao Tome
Population 179,506

Seychelles
Capital City Victoria
Population 89,188

South Africa
Capital Cities Bloemfontein, Cape Town and Tshwane (Pretoria)
Population 49,004,031

Swaziland
Capital City Mbabane
Population 1,370,424

Tanzania
Capital City Dodoma
Population 42,746,620

Uganda
Capital City Kampala
Population 34,612,250

Zambia
Capital City Lusaka
Population 13,881,336

Zimbabwe
Capital City Harare
Population 12,084,304

EUROPE
Northern Europe p.32

Denmark
Capital City Copenhagen
Population 5,529,888

Estonia
Capital City Tallinn
Population 1,282,963

Finland
Capital City Helsinki
Population 5,259,250

Iceland
Capital City Reykjavik
Population 311,058

Latvia
Capital City Riga
Population 2,204,708

Lithuania
Capital City Vilnius
Population 3,535,547

Norway
Capital City Oslo
Population 4,691,849

Sweden
Capital City Stockholm
Population 9,088,728

Western Europe p.34

Andorra
Capital City Andorra la Vella
Population 84,825

Belgium
Capital City Brussels
Population 10,431,477

France
Capital City Paris
Population 65,312,249

Ireland
Capital City Dublin
Population 4,670,976

Luxembourg
Capital City Luxembourg
Population 503,302

Monaco
Capital City Monaco-Ville
Population 30,539

Netherlands
Capital Cities Amsterdam and The Hague
Population 16,847,007

Portugal
Capital City Lisbon
Population 10,760,305

Spain
Capital City Madrid
Population 46,754,784

United Kingdom
Capital City London
Population 62,698,362

Central Europe p.36

Austria
Capital City Vienna
Population 8,217,280

Czech Republic
Capital City Prague
Population 10,190,213

Germany
Capital City Berlin
Population 81,471,834

Italy
Capital City Rome
Population 61,016,804

Liechtenstein
Capital City Vaduz
Population 35,236

Malta
Capital City Valletta
Population 408,333

Poland
Capital City Warsaw
Population 38,441,588

San Marino
Capital City San Marino
Population 31,817

Slovakia
Capital City Bratislava
Population 5,477,038

Slovenia
Capital City Ljubljana
Population 2,000,092

Switzerland
Capital City Bern
Population 7,639,961

Vatican City
Capital City Vatican City
Population 832

Southeast Europe p.38

Albania
Capital City Tirana
Population 2,994,667

Belarus
Capital City Minsk
Population 9,577,552

Bosnia and Herzegovina
Capital City Sarajevo
Population 4,622,163

Bulgaria
Capital City Sofia
Population 7,093,635

Croatia
Capital City Zagreb
Population 4,483,804

Greece
Capital City Athens
Population 10,760,136

Hungary
Capital City Budapest
Population 9,976,062

Kosovo
Capital City Pristina
Population 1,825,632

Macedonia
Capital City Skopje
Population 2,077,328

Moldova
Capital City Chisinau
Population 4,314,377

Montenegro
Capital City Podgorica
Population 661,807

Romania
Capital City Bucharest
Population 21,904,551

Serbia
Capital City Belgrade
Population 7,310,555

Ukraine
Capital City Kiev
Population 45,134,707

Russian Federation p.40

Russian Federation
Capital City Moscow
Population 138,739,892

ASIA
Southwest Asia p.42

Armenia
Capital City Yerevan
Population 2,967,975

Azerbaijan
Capital City Baku
Population 8,372,373

Bahrain
Capital City Manama
Population 1,214,705

Cyprus
Capital City Nicosia
Population 1,120,489

Georgia
Capital City T'bilisi
Population 4,585,874

Iran
Capital City Tehran
Population 77,891,220

Iraq
Capital City Baghdad
Population 30,399,572

Israel
Capital City Jerusalem
Population 7,473,052

Jordan
Capital City Amman
Population 6,508,271

Kuwait
Capital City Kuwait
Population 2,595,628

Lebanon
Capital City Beirut
Population 4,143,101

Oman
Capital City Muscat
Population 3,027,959

Qatar
Capital City Doha
Population 848,016

Saudi Arabia
Capital City Riyadh
Population 26,131,703

Syria
Capital City Damascus
Population 22,517,750

Turkey
Capital City Ankara
Population 78,785,548

United Arab Emirates
Capital City Abu Dhabi
Population 5,148,664

Yemen
Capital City Sana
Population 24,133,492

Central Asia p.44

Afghanistan
Capital City Kabul
Population 29,835,392

Kazakhstan
Capital City Astana
Population 15,522,373

Kyrgyzstan
Capital City Bishkek
Population 5,587,443

Tajikistan
Capital City Dushanbe
Population 7,627,200

Turkmenistan
Capital City Asgabat
Population 4,997,503

Uzbekistan
Capital City Tashkent
Population 28,128,600

South Asia p.46

Bangladesh
Capital City Dhaka
Population 158,570,535

Bhutan
Capital City Thimphu
Population 708,427

India
Capital City New Delhi
Population 1,189,172,906

Maldives
Capital City Male
Population 394,999

Nepal
Capital City Kathmandu
Population 29,391,883

Pakistan
Capital City Islamabad
Population 187,342,721

Sri Lanka
Capital City Colombo
Population 21,283,913

East Asia p.48

 China
Capital City Beijing
Population 1,336,718,015

Japan
Capital City Tokyo
Population 126,475,664

Mongolia
Capital City Ulan Bator
Population 3,133,318

North Korea
Capital City Pyongyang
Population 24,051,218

South Korea
Capital City Seoul
Population 48,754,657

Taiwan
Capital City Taipei
Population 23,071,779

Southeast Asia p50

Brunei
Capital City Bandar Seri Begawan
Population 401,890

Burma
Capital City Naypyidaw
Population 53,500,000

Cambodia
Capital City Phnom Penh
Population 14,701,717

East Timor
Capital City Dili
Population 1,177,834

Indonesia
Capital City Jakarta
Population 245,613,043

Laos
Capital City Vientiane
Population 6,477,211

Malaysia
Capital City Kuala Lumpur
Population 28,728,607

Philippines
Capital City Manila
Population 101,833,938

Singapore
Capital City Singapore
Population 4,740,737

Thailand
Capital City Bangkok
Population 66,720,153

Vietnam
Capital City Ha Noi
Population 90,549,390

AUSTRALASIA AND OCEANIA
Australia p.52

Australia
Capital City Canberra
Population 21,766,711

Pacific Islands p.54

Fiji
Capital City Suva
Population 883,125

Kiribati
Capital City Bairiki
Population 100,743

Marshall Islands
Capital City Majuro
Population 67,182

Micronesia
Capital City Palikir
Population 106,836

Nauru
Capital City no official capital
Population 9,322

Palau
Capital City Ngerulmud (Melekeok)
Population 20,956

Papua New Guinea
Capital City Port Moresby
Population 6,187,591

Samoa
Capital City Apia
Population 193,161

Solomon Islands
Capital City Honiara
Population 571,890

Tonga
Capital City Nuku'alofa
Population 105,916

Tuvalu
Capital City Funafuti
Population 10,544

Vanuatu
Capital City Port-Vila
Population 224,564

New Zealand p.56

New Zealand
Capital City Wellington
Population 4,290,347

ANTARCTICA p.59
The continent of Antarctica is unusual because it does not have any countries and no-one lives there all year round.

Canada

NORTH AMERICA

This is the second biggest country in the world (the largest is the Russian Federation), and it is part of North America. In southern Canada, wheat and other crops grow on the Great Plains. Farther north are thick coniferous forests and many rivers and lakes. Near the Arctic Circle, in the north, is a huge area of tundra, which turns marshy in summer, and inside the Arctic Circle the ground is always frozen. Most of the 34 million people in Canada live in the south, within 100 miles of the border with the USA. The weather is milder there and traveling is easier. The population is made up mostly of the descendants of Europeans who settled there from the 16th century, plus the original First Nations people. Canada is rich in minerals and fossil fuels, and mining is an important industry. Other industries are fishing, agriculture, machinery, car, timber, and paper manufacturing.

Country File

Canada

The maple leaf is the national symbol of Canada.

ARCTIC OCEAN

Beaufort Sea

Banks Island

Que

Victo Islan

UNITED STATES OF AMERICA (Alaska)

Arctic Circle

Yukon

MACKENZIE MOUNTAINS

Mackenzie

Great Bear Lake

Mount Logan 19,551 ft ▲

YUKON TERRITORY

NORTHWEST TERRITORIES

★ Whitehorse

★ Yellowknife

Great Slave Lake

C

A

N

Lake Athabasca

Peace

ROCKY MOUNTAINS

Reindeer Lake

Queen Charlotte Islands

BRITISH

Prince George ●

C

ALBERTA

G R E A T

COLUMBIA

Athabasca

SASKATCHEWAN

Fraser

Edmonton ★

Saskatche

Vancouver Island

Kamloops ●

Red Deer ●

P L A I N S

Nanaimo ●

Vancouver ●

Kelowna ●

Calgary ●

● Saskatoon

Victoria ★

Lethbridge ●

Medicine Hat ●

★ Regina

UNITED STATES

N

Lakes and forests

There are thousands of freshwater lakes and rivers in Canada, and almost half of the country is covered in forest. Wood products, especially wood pulp and paper, make up a large part of Canada's export trade.

0	250	500 kilometers

0	250	500 m

Beaver

The American beaver is the largest rodent in North America and it can measure over 4 feet from nose to tail. Beavers build dams across rivers to form lakes, where they are safe from predators such as wolves and bears. Their dams are made from logs, sticks, and mud. Beavers then build homes in the lake called lodges.

1

Ellesmere Island

GREENLAND

2

...abeth Islands

Baffin Bay

Did you know?

◈ Ice hockey is one of the fastest-growing women's sports. In 2006 the Canadian women's ice hockey team won the Olympic gold medal. Then they were world champions in 2007 and runners-up for the next three years.

Salmon fishing

The cold waters around the coast of Canada are rich in fish, including cod and salmon. Salmon is very important to the Canadian fishing industry, and tinned salmon is exported around the world.

3

Baffin Island

Davis Strait

4

NUNAVUT

Did you know?

◈ Canada has two official languages – French and English.

◈ Canada produces more hydroelectricity than any other nation in the world, except China.

5

Iqaluit ★

Southampton Island

Hudson Strait

Labrador Sea

6

Ungava Bay

UNGAVA PENINSULA

Moose

A moose is over 6 feet tall at the shoulder and is the biggest deer in the world. It roams through most of Canada, eating young trees and shrubs. Its name cames from a Native American word, *mus* or *moos*, which means "twig eater."

Hudson Bay

A   D   A

NEWFOUNDLAND AND LABRADOR

7

Churchill

Smallwood Reservoir

MANITOBA

La Grande Reservoir

James Bay

QUÉBEC

LAURENTIAN MOUNTAINS

8

ONTARIO

Anticosti Island

Gulf of St. Lawrence

Newfoundland

St. John's ★

SAINT PIERRE & MIQUELON (to France)

Lake Winnipeg

SHIELD

PRINCE EDWARD ISLAND

9

Winnipeg

Lake Nipigon

Chicoutimi ●

NEW BRUNSWICK

★ Charlottetown

Fredericton ● ● Moncton

Thunder Bay ●

Québec ★

★ Saint John

AMERICA

Lake Superior

Sudbury ●

Trois-Rivières ●

St. Lawrence

Montreal ●

● Sherbrooke

Bay of Fundy

★ Halifax

NOVA SCOTIA

ATLANTIC OCEAN

Canada

10

Sault Ste Marie ●

Lake Huron

OTTAWA ★

Did you know?

◈ Lake Superior is the largest freshwater lake in the world by area. It is 32,151 square miles – almost as big as Austria.

◈ Canada is famous for maple syrup, which is made from the sap of the maple tree.

Lake Michigan

Toronto ★ Oshawa ●

Kitchener ● ● St. Catharines

London ● Hamilton ●

Lake Ontario

Niagara Falls

Windsor ●

Lake Erie

CN Tower

At over 1,815 feet high, Canada's National Tower in Toronto is the world's tallest free-standing tower. It is one of the greatest feats of engineering. From the top of the tower you can see as far as 99 miles away.

United States of America

NORTH AMERICA

The United States of America (U.S.A.) covers an area almost the size of Europe. It includes the states of Alaska at the northwest tip of Canada and Hawaii in the Pacific Ocean.

Country File

United States of America

The land and climate of the U.S.A. change dramatically across this huge area. There are deserts, mountains, prairie lands, and swamps. In Alaska there is permanent snow and temperatures drop to below -22°F in winter. In the southeast the temperature rarely drops below 50°F. The population of over 313 million contains people descended from immigrants from all over the world, especially Europe. There are also 2.5 million Native American people. The U.S.A. is one of the world's wealthiest nations. There are huge oil and gas fields in Texas and Oklahoma, minerals are mined in Montana and Wyoming, and California is a center for the computer industry. Some of the world's best wine is also made in California.

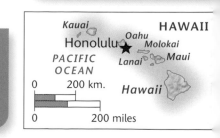

Detroit has been home to the U.S.A.'s motor industry since Henry Ford built his first vehicle there in 1896.

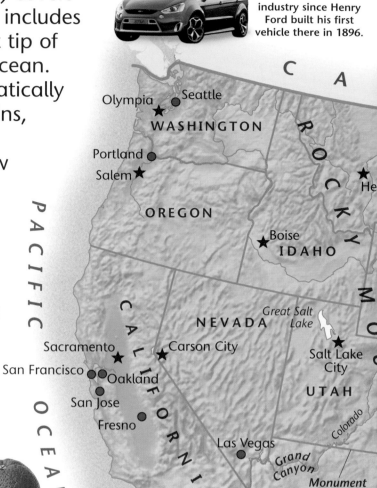

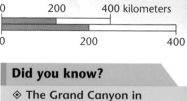

The sunny state of California produces half of the U.S.A.'s fruit and vegetables.

Monument Valley

The great "buttes" of Monument Valley, on the border of Utah and Arizona, were formed by rivers, rain, and wind, which have eroded the soft rock around them over millions of years. The land between the buttes was once as high as they are. Their red color comes from iron oxide in the soil, which is also known as rust.

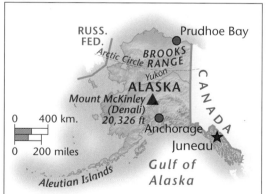

Did you know?

◆ The largest oil field in the U.S.A. is in Prudhoe Bay, Alaska. But the ground there is frozen for most of the year, which makes it difficult to drill for oil.

◆ The 16 highest mountains in the United States of America are all in Alaska.

Did you know?

◆ The Grand Canyon in Arizona is one of the natural wonders of the world. It is up to 5,905 feet deep and was cut out by the Colorado river over many millions of years.

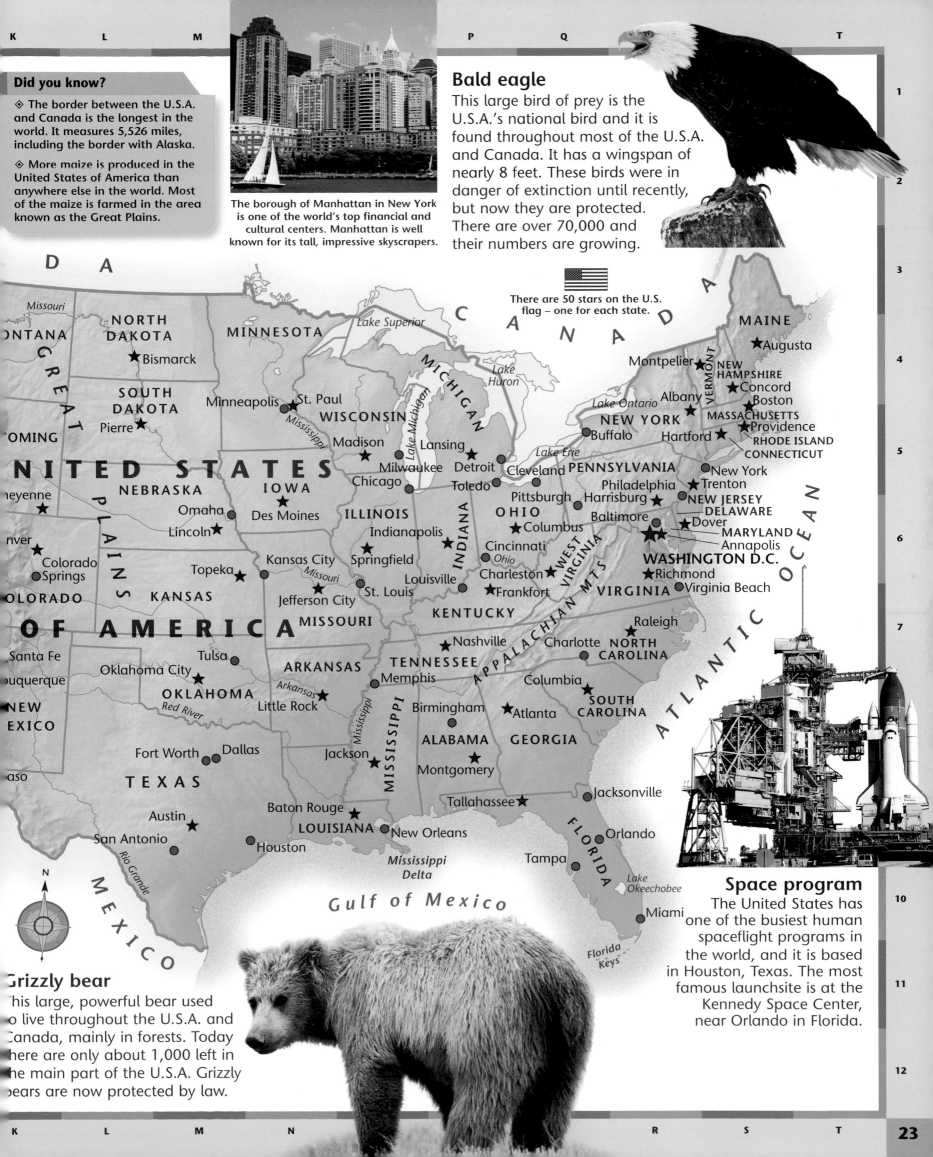

Did you know?

◇ The border between the U.S.A. and Canada is the longest in the world. It measures 5,526 miles, including the border with Alaska.

◇ More maize is produced in the United States of America than anywhere else in the world. Most of the maize is farmed in the area known as the Great Plains.

The borough of Manhattan in New York is one of the world's top financial and cultural centers. Manhattan is well known for its tall, impressive skyscrapers.

Bald eagle

This large bird of prey is the U.S.A.'s national bird and it is found throughout most of the U.S.A. and Canada. It has a wingspan of nearly 8 feet. These birds were in danger of extinction until recently, but now they are protected. There are over 70,000 and their numbers are growing.

There are 50 stars on the U.S. flag – one for each state.

CANADA

Missouri

NORTH DAKOTA
★ Bismarck

MINNESOTA
Lake Superior

MAINE
★ Augusta

MONTANA

SOUTH DAKOTA
Pierre ★

Minneapolis ● ★ St. Paul
Mississippi
WISCONSIN
Madison ★

Montpelier ● VERMONT ● NEW HAMPSHIRE
Lake Huron
Lake Ontario
Albany ★ ● Concord
● Boston
MASSACHUSETTS
★ Providence

WYOMING

Lansing ★
Milwaukee ●
Chicago ●
MICHIGAN

Buffalo ●
NEW YORK
Hartford ●
RHODE ISLAND
CONNECTICUT

UNITED STATES

NEBRASKA
Omaha ●
Lincoln ★

IOWA
Des Moines ★

Detroit ★
Toledo ●
Cleveland ●
PENNSYLVANIA
Pittsburgh ●
Harrisburg ●
New York ●
Trenton ★
Philadelphia ●
NEW JERSEY
DELAWARE
Dover ★

Cheyenne ★

ILLINOIS
Indianapolis ★
INDIANA
OHIO
Columbus ★
Cincinnati ●
Ohio
Baltimore ●
MARYLAND
Annapolis ●

Denver ★
Colorado Springs ●

Kansas City ●
Topeka ★
Missouri
Springfield ★
St. Louis ●
Louisville ●
Charleston ★
WEST VIRGINIA
Frankfort ★
WASHINGTON D.C.
★ Richmond
● Virginia Beach

COLORADO

KANSAS
Jefferson City ●
MISSOURI
KENTUCKY
VIRGINIA

OF AMERICA

Santa Fe ★
Tulsa ●
Nashville ★
Charlotte ●
Raleigh ★
NORTH CAROLINA

ALBUQUERQUE ●
Oklahoma City ★
ARKANSAS
Memphis ●
Columbia ●
SOUTH CAROLINA

NEW MEXICO
OKLAHOMA
Arkansas
Red River
Little Rock ★
Birmingham ●
Atlanta ★
APPALACHIAN MTS

El Paso

MISSISSIPPI
Jackson ★
ALABAMA
Montgomery ★
GEORGIA

Fort Worth ● ● Dallas

TEXAS
Baton Rouge ●
LOUISIANA ● New Orleans
Tallahassee ★
Jacksonville ●

Austin ★
San Antonio ●
Houston ●
FLORIDA
Orlando ●

Rio Grande

Mississippi Delta
Tampa ●
Lake Okeechobee

ATLANTIC OCEAN

MEXICO

Gulf of Mexico

Miami ●
Florida Keys

Space program

The United States has one of the busiest human spaceflight programs in the world, and it is based in Houston, Texas. The most famous launchsite is at the Kennedy Space Center, near Orlando in Florida.

Grizzly bear

This large, powerful bear used to live throughout the U.S.A. and Canada, mainly in forests. Today there are only about 1,000 left in the main part of the U.S.A. Grizzly bears are now protected by law.

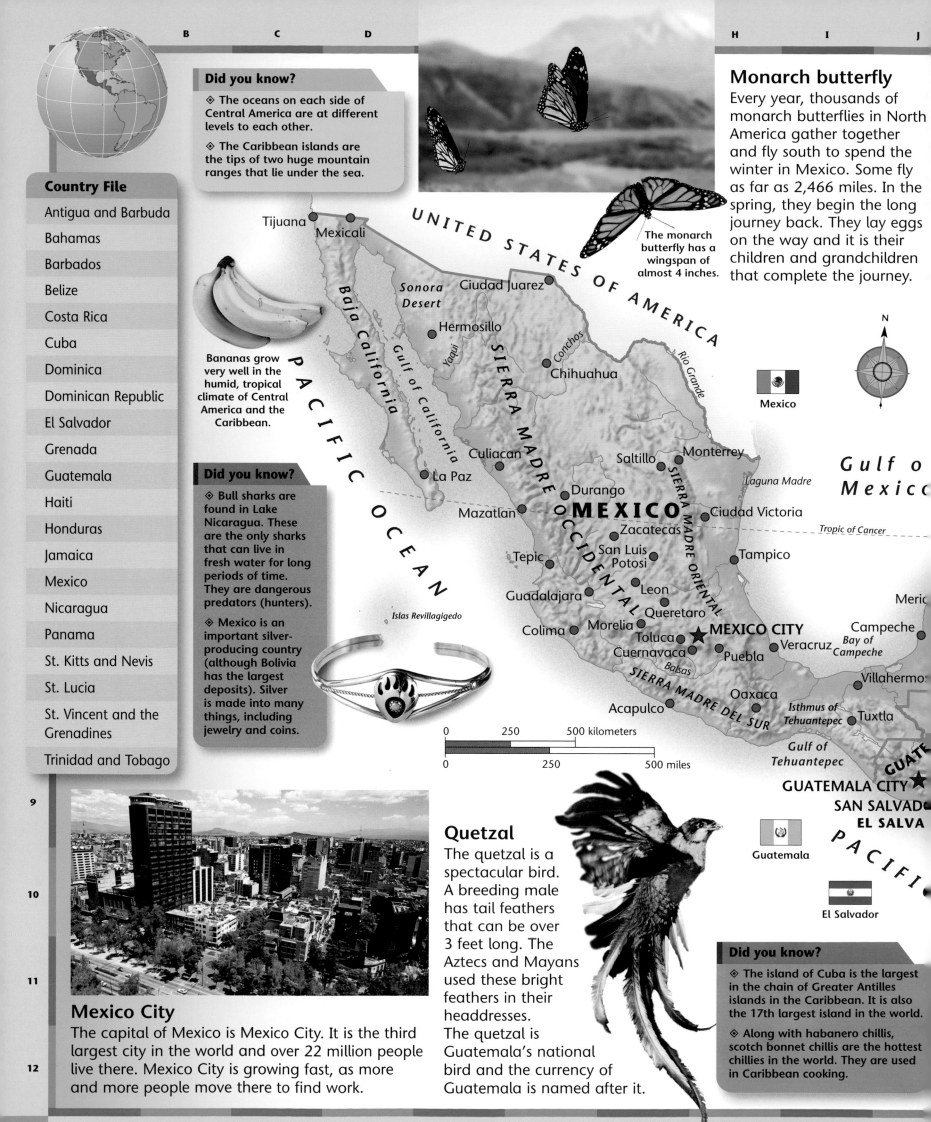

Did you know?

◊ The oceans on each side of Central America are at different levels to each other.

◊ The Caribbean islands are the tips of two huge mountain ranges that lie under the sea.

Monarch butterfly

Every year, thousands of monarch butterflies in North America gather together and fly south to spend the winter in Mexico. Some fly as far as 2,466 miles. In the spring, they begin the long journey back. They lay eggs on the way and it is their children and grandchildren that complete the journey.

The monarch butterfly has a wingspan of almost 4 inches.

Country File

Antigua and Barbuda

Bahamas

Barbados

Belize

Costa Rica

Cuba

Dominica

Dominican Republic

El Salvador

Grenada

Guatemala

Haiti

Honduras

Jamaica

Mexico

Nicaragua

Panama

St. Kitts and Nevis

St. Lucia

St. Vincent and the Grenadines

Trinidad and Tobago

Bananas grow very well in the humid, tropical climate of Central America and the Caribbean.

Did you know?

◊ Bull sharks are found in Lake Nicaragua. These are the only sharks that can live in fresh water for long periods of time. They are dangerous predators (hunters).

◊ Mexico is an important silver-producing country (although Bolivia has the largest deposits). Silver is made into many things, including jewelry and coins.

UNITED STATES OF AMERICA

Tijuana
Mexicali
Ciudad Juarez
Sonora Desert
Baja California
Hermosillo
Yaqui
Conchos
Rio Grande
Chihuahua
Gulf of California
SIERRA MADRE OCCIDENTAL
Culiacan
Saltillo
Monterrey
La Paz
Durango
SIERRA MADRE ORIENTAL
Laguna Madre
Mazatlan
MEXICO
Ciudad Victoria
Zacatecas
Tropic of Cancer
San Luis Potosi
Tampico
Tepic
Gulf of Mexico
Guadalajara
Leon
Colima
Morelia
Queretaro
Meri
Toluca
MEXICO CITY
Campeche
Cuernavaca
Puebla
Veracruz
Bay of Campeche
Balsas
Villahermos
SIERRA MADRE DEL SUR
Oaxaca
Acapulco
Isthmus of Tehuantepec
Tuxtla
Gulf of Tehuantepec
PACIFIC OCEAN
Islas Revillagigedo

Mexico

N

GUATE
GUATEMALA CITY
SAN SALVADO
EL SALVA
PACIFI

Guatemala

El Salvador

0   250   500 kilometers
0   250   500 miles

Mexico City

The capital of Mexico is Mexico City. It is the third largest city in the world and over 22 million people live there. Mexico City is growing fast, as more and more people move there to find work.

Quetzal

The quetzal is a spectacular bird. A breeding male has tail feathers that can be over 3 feet long. The Aztecs and Mayans used these bright feathers in their headdresses. The quetzal is Guatemala's national bird and the currency of Guatemala is named after it.

Did you know?

◊ The island of Cuba is the largest in the chain of Greater Antilles islands in the Caribbean. It is also the 17th largest island in the world.

◊ Along with habanero chillis, scotch bonnet chillis are the hottest chillies in the world. They are used in Caribbean cooking.

Central America and the Caribbean
NORTH AMERICA

The continents of North and South America are linked by a narrow piece of land called Central America. To the east are the Greater and Lesser Antilles islands, which are also known as the Caribbean islands. All along Central America there are mountains and volcanoes. In the north there are hot, dry deserts and in the south there are tropical rain forests. The Caribbean also has rain forests and a tropical climate. Most of the people who live in this region are descended from Africans, Asians, and Europeans. In Central America, fishing, coffee, and fruit growing are important industries, and most of Mexico's income comes from oil and gas. Tourism and sugar farming are important in the Caribbean.

Caribbean islands
St. Lucia, Antigua, and the other islands of the Caribbean are popular holiday destinations. Many tourists are attracted by the warm, clear sea, sandy beaches, and tropical climate.

Panama Canal
The Pacific and Atlantic Oceans are linked by the Panama Canal. This waterway is almost 50 miles long. By using the canal, a boat traveling from one coast of North America to the other can avoid going around Cape Horn in South America and cut its journey by around 9,320 miles.

South America

SOUTH AMERICA

The continent of South America is home to the Amazon rain forest and mountains of the Andes. The Amazon River is over 4,000 miles long and is the greatest river in South America. The climate ranges from tropical in the north to bitterly cold in the south – the tip of South America is only around 621 miles away from Antarctica. In between, the climate is less extreme. There are wide, open grasslands called the Pampas, where cattle and cereals are farmed. Northern South America is rich in oil and gas, especially in Venezuela. Farther south, copper and iron ore are found. Coffee is the most important crop in South America, and Brazil is the world's leading coffee grower. Cocoa, sugarcane, and bananas are also important crops. Most of the population is descended from Europeans, Amerindians, or Africans.

Country File

- Argentina
- Bolivia
- Brazil
- Chile
- Colombia
- Ecuador
- Guyana
- Paraguay
- Peru
- Suriname
- Uruguay
- Venezuela

6

Angel Falls

The highest waterfall in the world is the Angel Falls in Venezuela. Angel Falls is over 3,280 feet high – 19 times higher than the Niagara Falls on the U.S. and Canada border.

Did you know?

◇ Bolivia has two capital cities – La Paz and Sucre. La Paz is 11,811 feet above sea level, which makes it the highest capital city in the world.

◇ Ecuador exports more bananas than any other country in the world.

◇ The Amazon rain forest is over half the size of the United States of America.

◇ The grass in the Pampas region grows up to 9 feet tall. It has long, thin, sharp, leaves and big, fluffy flowerheads.

Many of the best known vegetables in the world, such as tomatoes, potatoes, beans and sweetcorn, originally came from South America.

Carnival time

Every year, just before Lent, "Carnival" begins in Rio de Janeiro, Brazil. For five days people dress up, dance, and parade through the streets to the sound of samba music. There is a competition for the most outrageous costume and the best decorated float.

Amazon rain forest

10

11

12

The Amazon rain forest is the largest tropical rain forest in the world. Many scientists believe that more than one-third of all the world's species of plants and animals live there. About 0.6 square miles of Brazilian rain forest are being destroyed every hour, as the forest is cut down for timber and cleared for farming. If this continues, the rain forest will eventually be gone. Hundreds of thousands of species of animals and plants will be lost for ever.

Jaguar

For its size, the jaguar is one of the strongest mammals in the world. This cat can kill prey over three times its own body weight. It is good at climbing, crawling, and swimming, which are useful skills in its rain forest habitat.

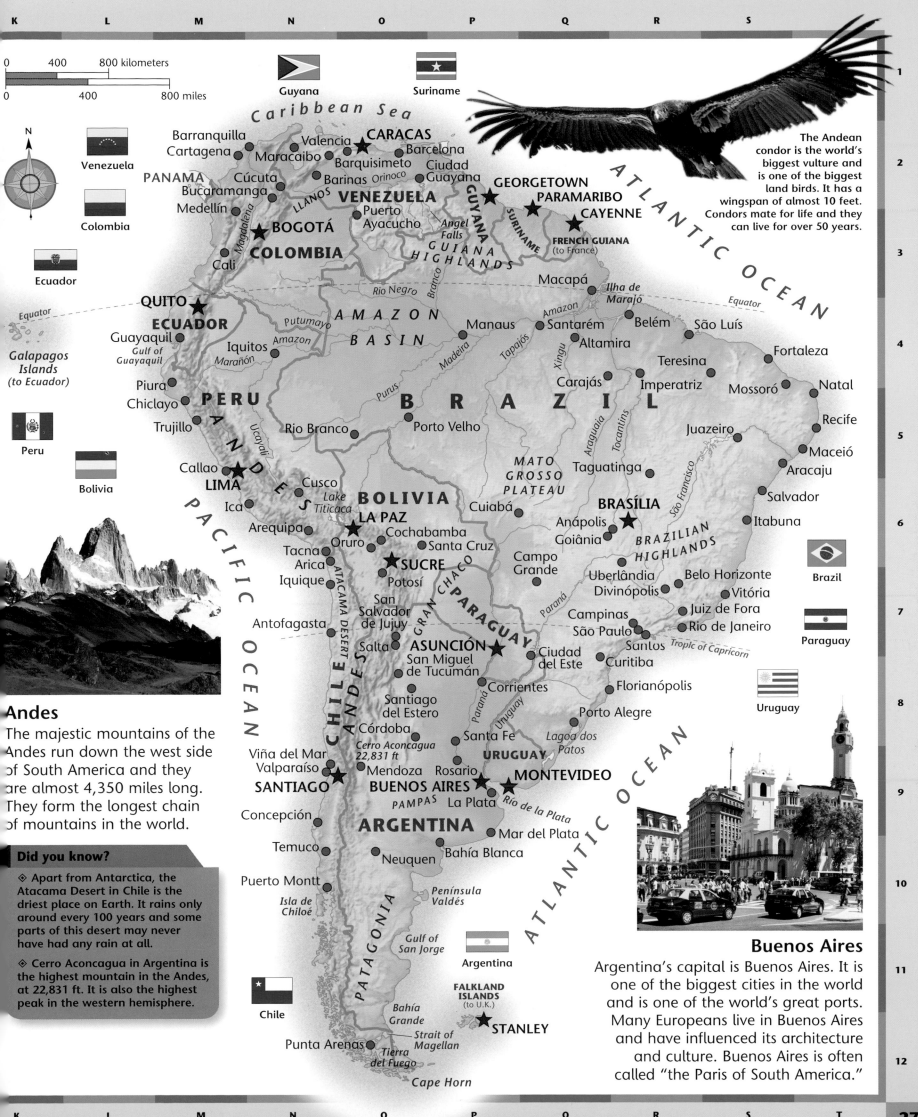

K L M N O P Q R S

0   400   800 kilometers
0   400   800 miles

N

Venezuela

Colombia

Ecuador

Peru

Bolivia

Guyana

Suriname

Caribbean Sea

Barranquilla
Cartagena
Valencia
CARACAS
Barcelona
Maracaibo
Barquisimeto
Ciudad
Cúcuta
Barinas
Orinoco
Guayana
PANAMA
Bucaramanga
VENEZUELA
GEORGETOWN
PARAMARIBO
Medellín
Puerto
Ayacucho
GUYANA
CAYENNE
BOGOTÁ
SURINAME
COLOMBIA
Angel Falls
FRENCH GUIANA (to France)
Cali
GUIANA HIGHLANDS

Rio Negro
Macapá
Ilha de Marajó
Equator

ATLANTIC OCEAN

QUITO
Equator
ECUADOR
A M A Z O N
Amazon
Putumayo
Manaus
Santarém
Belém
São Luís
Guayaquil
B A S I N
Fortaleza
Gulf of Guayaquil
Iquitos
Amazon
Altamira
Galapagos Islands (to Ecuador)
Marañón
Madeira
Teresina
Piura
Purus
Tapajós
Xingu
Carajás
Imperatriz
Mossoró
Natal
Chiclayo
PERU
B R A Z I L
Trujillo
Ucayali
Rio Branco
Porto Velho
Recife
Juazeiro
Maceió
Callao
Cusco
MATO GROSSO PLATEAU
Taguatinga
Aracaju
LIMA
BOLIVIA
São Francisco
Salvador
Ica
Lake Titicaca
Cuiabá
BRASÍLIA
Itabuna
Arequipa
LA PAZ
Anápolis
Tacna
Oruro
Cochabamba
Goiânia
BRAZILIAN HIGHLANDS
Arica
Santa Cruz
Campo
Uberlândia
Belo Horizonte
Iquique
SUCRE
Grande
Divinópolis
Vitória
Potosí
Araguaia
Tocantins
Juiz de Fora
Antofagasta
San Salvador de Jujuy
GRAN CHACO
PARAGUAY
Paraná
Campinas
Rio de Janeiro
Salta
São Paulo
Santos
Tropic of Capricorn
ASUNCIÓN
Ciudad del Este
Curitiba
San Miguel de Tucumán
Corrientes
Florianópolis
Paraná
Uruguay
Santiago del Estero
Porto Alegre
Córdoba
Santa Fe
Lagoa dos Patos
Cerro Aconcagua 22,831 ft
URUGUAY
Viña del Mar
Mendoza
Rosario
MONTEVIDEO
Valparaíso
BUENOS AIRES
SANTIAGO
PAMPAS
La Plata
Río de la Plata
Concepción
ARGENTINA
Mar del Plata
Temuco
Neuquen
Bahía Blanca
Puerto Montt
Península Valdés
Isla de Chiloé
Gulf of San Jorge
Argentina
PATAGONIA
Chile
FALKLAND ISLANDS (to U.K.)
Bahía Grande
STANLEY
Punta Arenas
Strait of Magellan
Tierra del Fuego
Cape Horn

Brazil

Paraguay

Uruguay

The Andean condor is the world's biggest vulture and is one of the biggest land birds. It has a wingspan of almost 10 feet. Condors mate for life and they can live for over 50 years.

Andes

The majestic mountains of the Andes run down the west side of South America and they are almost 4,350 miles long. They form the longest chain of mountains in the world.

Did you know?

◇ Apart from Antarctica, the Atacama Desert in Chile is the driest place on Earth. It rains only around every 100 years and some parts of this desert may never have had any rain at all.

◇ Cerro Aconcagua in Argentina is the highest mountain in the Andes, at 22,831 ft. It is also the highest peak in the western hemisphere.

Buenos Aires

Argentina's capital is Buenos Aires. It is one of the biggest cities in the world and is one of the world's great ports. Many Europeans live in Buenos Aires and have influenced its architecture and culture. Buenos Aires is often called "the Paris of South America."

Northern Africa

AFRICA

The continent of Africa is the second largest in the world (Asia is the biggest). Northern Africa is mostly covered by the Sahara, which is the world's largest hot desert. Few people live there because conditions are so harsh. Most people in Northern Africa live near the coast or along the River Nile. Crops such as dates, cork, grapes, and olives are produced in the north of the region, and cocoa, groundnuts (peanuts), and palm oil in the south. Textiles are made in every area, especially in the north, where rugs are produced. There are big deposits of oil and natural gas in Libya, and in countries such as Egypt, Tunisia, and Morocco, tourism is important.

Country File

Algeria

Benin

Burkina Faso

Cameroon

Cape Verde

Central African Republic

Chad

Djibouti

Egypt

Eritrea

Ethiopia

Gambia

Ghana

Guinea

Guinea-Bissau

Ivory Coast

Liberia

Libya

Mali

Mauritania

Morocco

Niger

Nigeria

Senegal

Sierra Leone

Somalia

South Sudan

Sudan

Togo

Tunisia

Western Sahara

Did you know?

◇ Uranium, diamonds, and gold are mined in northern Africa. There are also reserves of oil and natural gas in this area.

Did you know?

◇ Half of the world's cocoa beans are now grown in Northern Africa, even though the cocoa bean originally came from South America.

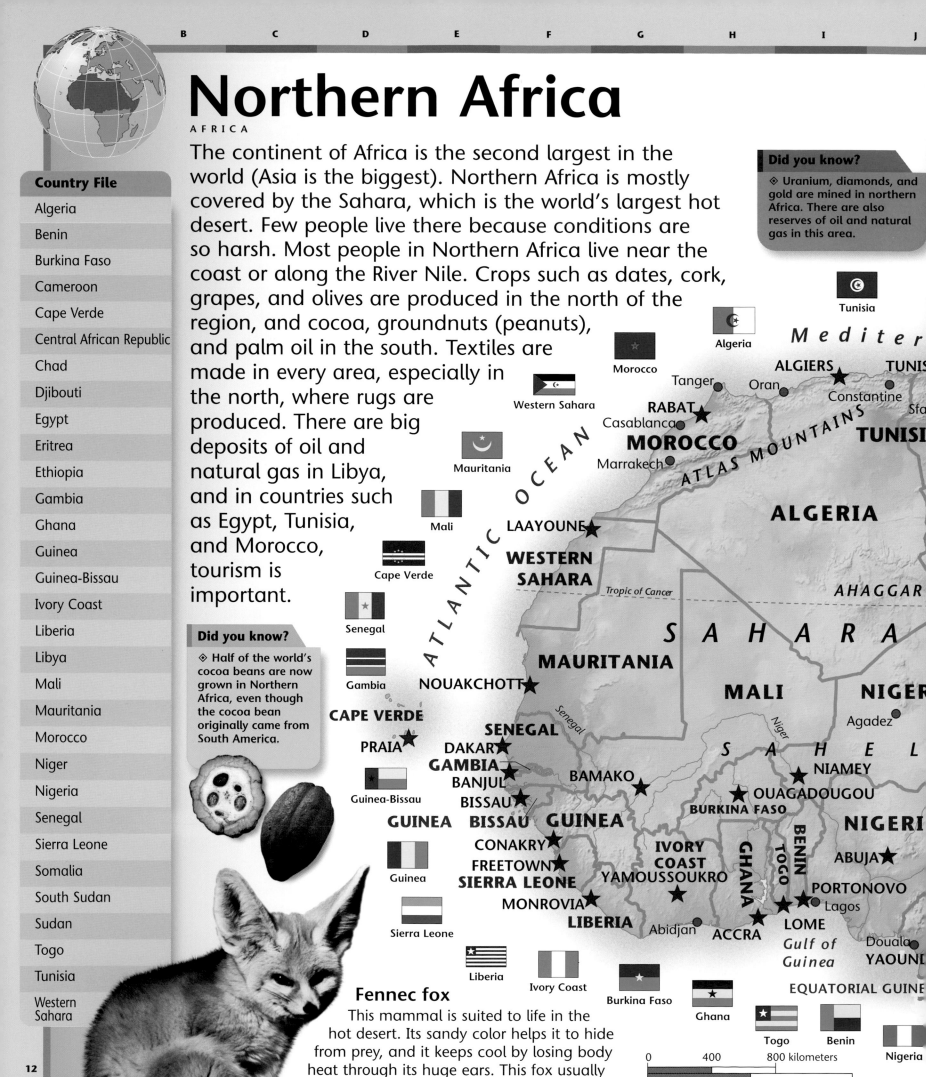

Fennec fox

This mammal is suited to life in the hot desert. Its sandy color helps it to hide from prey, and it keeps cool by losing body heat through its huge ears. This fox usually hunts at night when it is cooler.

0   400   800 kilometers

0   400   800 miles

12

Did you know?

◆ Cairo is the largest city in Africa and the capital of Egypt. Almost 17.3 million people live in this ancient city and its suburbs.

◆ In Niger, the average number of children in a family is seven.

Groundnuts (peanuts) are grown along the southern coast of northern Africa. Most of these nuts are made into cooking oil.

Sahara Desert

Strong winds in the Sahara blow the sand into dunes over 1,411 feet high. The desert is getting bigger because the winds blow the sand and because people have cut down trees around the edges for fuel and to grow crops. In the south, people are planting grasses to try to stop the desert from spreading any farther.

Did you know?

◆ Temperatures in the Sahara can range from below freezing at night to over 104°F during the day. Less than 1 inch of rain falls in a year.

◆ "Sahara" is Arabic for desert.

Did you know?

◆ Egypt grows more dates than anywhere else in the world. Archaeologists have found 7,000-year-old date stones in Egypt.

Scorpion

These creatures are found throughout northern Africa and are perfectly suited to desert life. Their hard, flat bodies protect them from the extremes of temperature and allow them to creep under rocks to hide from predators and the hot desert sun.

River Nile

At over 4,132 miles long, the Nile is the longest river in the world. It flows to the Nile Delta and into the Mediterranean Sea. Ninety-nine percent of the people living in Egypt live and work in the Nile delta and along the banks of the river.

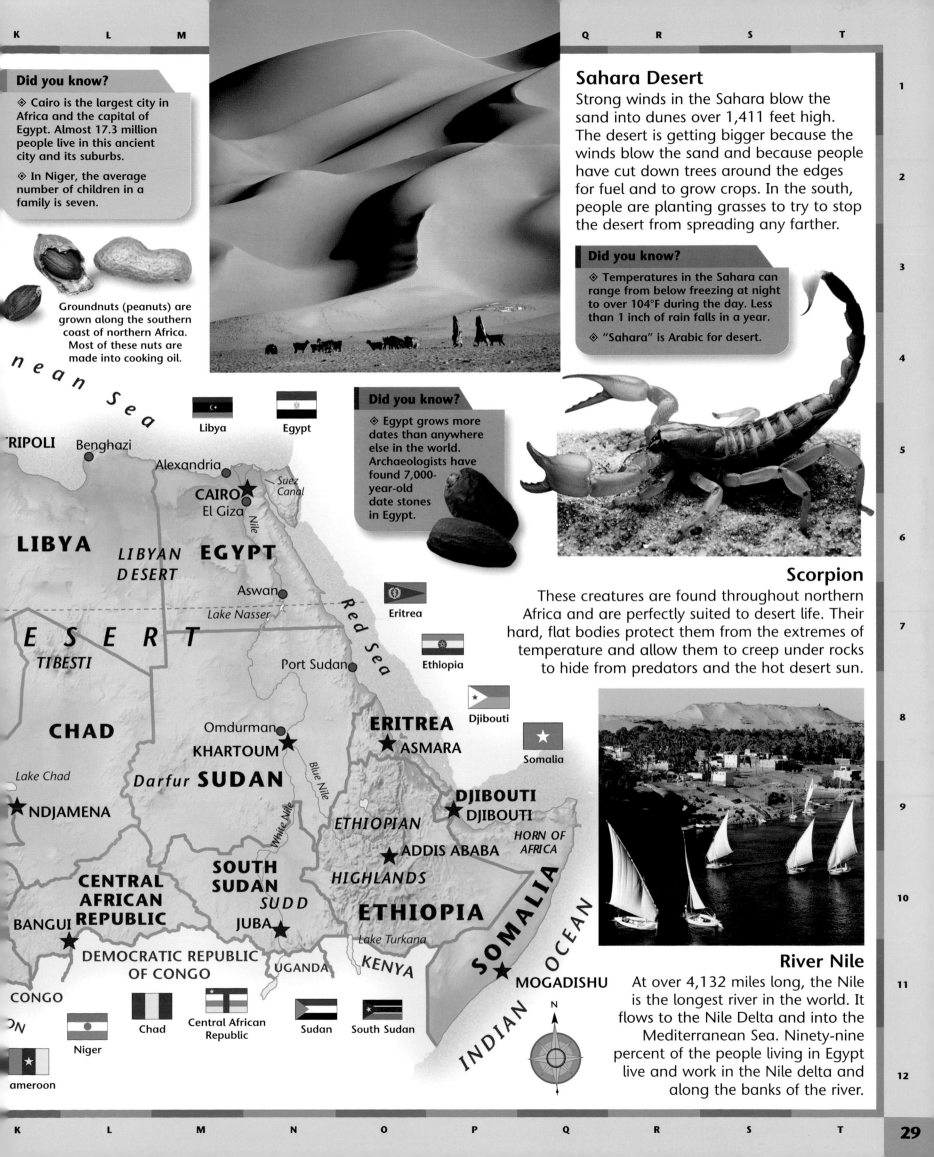

Map labels:
nean Sea

TRIPOLI Benghazi

Libya Egypt

Alexandria
CAIRO Suez Canal
El Giza
Nile

Eritrea

Ethiopia

LIBYA LIBYAN DESERT EGYPT

Aswan
Lake Nasser
Red Sea

ESERT
TIBESTI

Port Sudan

Djibouti

CHAD

Omdurman
KHARTOUM
ERITREA
ASMARA

Somalia

Lake Chad
Darfur SUDAN
Blue Nile

NDJAMENA

DJIBOUTI
DJIBOUTI

ETHIOPIAN
HORN OF AFRICA

White Nile

CENTRAL AFRICAN REPUBLIC
SOUTH SUDAN
SUDD
ADDIS ABABA
HIGHLANDS

BANGUI
JUBA
ETHIOPIA
SOMALIA

DEMOCRATIC REPUBLIC OF CONGO
UGANDA KENYA
Lake Turkana

CONGO
MOGADISHU

Chad Central African Republic Sudan South Sudan

Niger

INDIAN OCEAN
N

Cameroon

Southern Africa

AFRICA

Southern Africa has many different climates. The Congo Basin is hot and humid and is the site of the world's second biggest tropical rain forest (the Amazon forest in South America is the largest). Farther east and south are dry woodlands merging into savannah, which is a mixture of grassland and open woodland. It is there that the most well-known African animals are found. Farther south is the Namib Desert, one of the hottest and driest places on Earth, with temperatures over 122°F during the day. Hundreds of different tribes live in southern Africa, and there are hundreds of languages. The Kalahari Desert in Botswana is home to one of the few remaining groups of hunter gatherers, the Bushmen, or San. In the 19th century, large gold and diamond deposits were found in South Africa, helping it to become the most powerful country in Southern Africa.

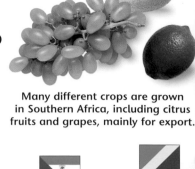

Many different crops are grown in Southern Africa, including citrus fruits and grapes, mainly for export.

Country File

Angola

Botswana

Burundi

Comoros

Congo

Democratic Republic of Congo

Equatorial Guinea

Gabon

Kenya

Lesotho

Madagascar

Malawi

Mauritius

Mozambique

Namibia

Rwanda

Sao Tome and Principe

Seychelles

South Africa

Swaziland

Tanzania

Uganda

Zambia

Zimbabwe

Victoria Falls

This famous waterfall is on the Zambezi River, on the border between Zambia and Zimbabwe. It is over 354 feet high and over 5,577 feet wide. David Livingstone was the first European to see it, in 1855. He named it for Queen Victoria of England. Local people call it "the smoke that thunders" because of the loud noise and spray that it makes.

Did you know?

◇ There are two species of elephant in Africa. The African bush elephant lives on the savannah and the smaller forest elephant lives in tropical rain forests.

◇ Half of all the world's diamonds are mined in Southern Africa.

African wildlife

Elephants, rhinoceroses, lions, leopards, and buffalo are known as "the big five" and they attract thousands of tourists to Africa. These animals used to be shot for sport and were the five most dangerous animals, but now they are shot with cameras! Many are endangered species and they are protected by law.

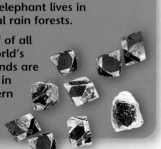

Equatorial Guinea

Congo

MALABO

CAMEROON

CENTRAL AFR

Ub

EQUATORIAL GUINEA

SAO TOME

Mbandaka

CO
BA

SAO TOME & PRINCIPE

LIBREVILLE

GABON

CONGO

Congo

DE
RE

Sao Tome and Principe

BRAZZAVILLE

KINSHAS

ANGOLA

Gabon

LUANDA

Angola

ANGOLA

Huambo

BIÉ
PLATEAU

Kana

Namibe

Lubango

Okava

NAMIBIA

WINDHOE

KALAH

DESE

Orange Riv

Namibia

Botswana

SO

CAPE TOWN

Cape of Good Hope

South Africa

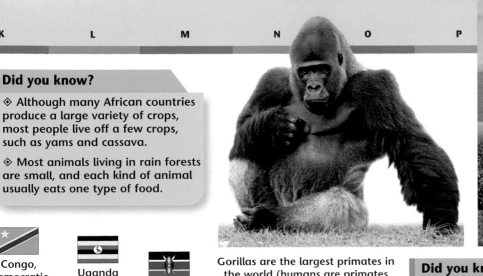

Did you know?

◈ Although many African countries produce a large variety of crops, most people live off a few crops, such as yams and cassava.

◈ Most animals living in rain forests are small, and each kind of animal usually eats one type of food.

Congo, Democratic Republic of

Uganda

Kenya

Gorillas are the largest primates in the world (humans are primates too). These apes live in forests, in groups led by a large male.

Did you know?

◈ The book (and film) *Gorillas in the Mist* is about rare mountain gorillas in Rwanda. It is by Dian Fossey, a zoologist who died trying to protect gorillas in the wild.

◈ The Okavango River never reaches the sea. Instead, its waters flood a huge area in northern Botswana called the Okavango Delta. This area is full of wildlife.

Kilimanjaro

The top of Kilimanjaro in Tanzania is covered in snow all year round, even though the mountain is close to the Equator. This is because the temperature drops as the land gets higher. Kilimanjaro is 19,341 feet high and it is the highest point in Africa.

Rwanda

Burundi

Tanzania

Seychelles

Comoros

Malawi

Zambia

Mauritius

MAYOTTE (to France)

Madagascar

Zimbabwe

Swaziland

Mozambique

Baobab tree

The island of Madagascar, off the eastern coast of Africa, split off from the mainland millions of years ago. Many unusual species of plants and animals developed there, and it is the only place on Earth where certain species of plants and animals can be found. Several types of baobab tree grow only in Madagascar. Some of these extraordinary trees are over 3,000 years old.

Did you know?

◈ The earliest known human fossils were found in the Olduvai Gorge in the Great Rift Valley in Tanzania. They are about 2.3 million years old. Many people think that this is where humans first evolved. The gorge is often called "the cradle of mankind."

South Africa's climate is varied and is suitable for growing many types of cut flower, such as gerberas (shown here), roses, and carnations. These are all exported to Europe, as well as being sold locally.

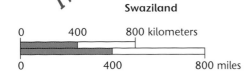
Lesotho

0 400 800 kilometers
0 400 800 miles

Northern Europe

EUROPE

Norway, Sweden, and Denmark are known as Scandinavia. The countries of Estonia, Latvia, and Lithuania are called the Baltic States. These six countries, together with Finland and Iceland, are the most northern ones in Europe. During the long, cold winters the sun rises for only a few hours each day. Most people in Scandinavia live in the cities or towns in the south and around the coast. Throughout Scandinavia there are forests, and many of the trees are used to make furniture and paper. Iron ore is used for making steel, and the water from the lakes and rivers produces electricity in hydroelectric power stations. There are plenty of fish in the coastal waters of northern Europe, and all these countries have strong fishing industries.

Country File

Denmark

Estonia

Finland

Iceland

Latvia

Lithuania

Norway

Sweden

Lapland

The northern part of Norway, Sweden, and Finland is known as Lapland. This is the home of the Sami people. They are descended from nomadic people who lived in northern Scandinavia for thousands of years. Some Sami still herd reindeer, which they keep for their milk, meat, and skins.

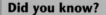

Red squirrel

The red squirrel lives all over northern Europe. Although it is called "red" it can be black, brown, or red with a pale belly. Other mammals, such as brown bears, elk, and gray wolves, are also found in the forests of Scandinavia.

Did you know?

◈ Finland has more than 188,000 lakes and three-quarters of the country is covered by forest.

◈ Norway was rated the world's most peaceful country on the 2007 Global Peace Index.

◈ About a third of all Estonians live in Estonia's capital city, Tallinn.

Did you know?

◈ Denmark has some of the longest beaches in the whole of Europe.

◈ Many English words come from Scandinavian languages. The word "garden" means farm in Danish, and gardens in medieval England used to be full of vegetables!

Two-thirds of the land in Denmark is used for farming. Most of it is used for pig farming or for growing food for the pigs.

Norwegian fjords

Fjords are long, deep, steep-sided valleys, which glaciers carved through the mountains over 150,000 years ago. As the ice melted, the sea levels rose and the valleys flooded with water. Thousands of tourists visit the fjords each year to enjoy the beautiful scenery.

Timber for building

Wood is a very important material for all of the countries in northern Europe. Over the centuries wood has been used for producing fuel, for making furniture and toys, and for building houses and churches. There are so many trees in this area that many houses and public buildings are still made from wood today.

ARCTIC OCEAN

North Cape

Barents Sea

Hammerfest

ICELAND

Greenland Sea   *Arctic Circle*

Akureyri

REYKJAVIK   *Vatnajokull*

Strokkur Geyser

ATLANTIC OCEAN

0   100 km.
0   100 miles

FAEROE ISLANDS
(to Denmark)

Torshavn

0   20 km.
0   20 miles

Norway

Iceland

Tromso

Norwegian Sea

Narvik

LAPLAND

Bodo

Kebnekaise
2117m

Arctic Circle

Ounasjoki

Kemijoki

Lulea

Oulu

Finland

Trondheim

Ostersund

Umea

Vaasa

Kuopio

Jyvaskyla

Saimaa

N O R W A Y   S W E D E N   F I N L A N D

Sognefjorden

Lillehammer

Glama

Klaralven

Dalalven

Tampere

Lahti

Gulf of Bothnia

ergen

Drammen   **OSLO**
Moss

Skien

Stavanger

Kristiansand

Skagerrak

Gavle

Uppsala

Vasteras

Orebro

STOCKHOLM

Norrkoping

Linkoping

Vanern

Vattern

Gothenburg

Jonkoping

Aland Islands

Turku

Vantaa
HELSINKI
Espoo

Gulf of Finland

TALLINN

Hiiumaa

Estonia

Lake Peipus

ESTONIA

Tartu

Saaremaa

Gulf of Riga

LATVIA

Gotland

Liepaja

RIGA   *Western Dvina*

Daugavpils

Oland

orth Sea

Aalborg

Kattegat

DENMARK

Arhus

Helsingborg

COPENHAGEN
Odense   Malmo

Bornholm

Baltic Sea

Klaipeda

LITHUANIA

Neman

Kaunas

VILNIUS

RUSSIAN FEDERATION (Kaliningrad)

RUSSIAN FEDERATION

BELARUS

Denmark

Sweden

G E R M A N Y   P O L A N D

100   200 kilometers
100   200 mile

Lithuania

Latvia

R U S S I A N   F E D E R A T I O N

33

Western Europe

EUROPE

The area in Europe that is farthest from Asia is known as western Europe. The most northern countries have a mild, wet climate. Farther south the climate becomes increasingly warmer. In southern France, Spain, and Portugal, the temperature in summer often reaches over 86°F. The land is suitable for many kinds of farming. Oranges are grown in Spain, flowers in the Netherlands, and wheat and potatoes are grown throughout western Europe. Many countries also grow grapes to make wine. Wine-making is important in France, Spain, and Portugal. Most people in western Europe live in large towns and cities. This region is very popular with holiday-makers, and tourism is a big industry. Electronics and car manufacturing are also major industries in western Europe.

Country File

Andorra

Belgium

France

Ireland

Luxembourg

Monaco

Netherlands

Portugal

Spain

United Kingdom

Red fox

Foxes are members of the dog family. They are found all across Europe and survive in towns and cities as well as the countryside. They eat all kinds of things, such as worms, berries, insects, small mammals, and household waste.

Did you know?

◇ Three countries in Europe are called principalities, which means that they are reigned over by a prince or princess. They are Andorra, Liechtenstein, and Monaco.

The French TGV "*Train à Grande Vitesse,*" travels at an average speed of 186 mph. The TGV can carry 377 passengers. It is the fastest train in Europe.

Did you know?

◇ People in Andorra live the longest lives in the world, at an average of 83.5 years.

◇ People from South America, Indonesia, and the Caribbean make up five percent of the population of the Netherlands. There used to be Dutch colonies in these places.

Over 500 different varieties of cheese are made in France, including Brie and Roquefort.

Costa Brava

The coastal region in northeast Spain known as the Costa Brava stretches for around 99 miles along the Mediterranean Sea. It is popular for its sandy beaches and its warm seas. The area is also an important cork-growing region and supplies cork to wine producers all over the world.

London Eye

Millions of tourists visit London every year for its history, theaters, and sights, such as Big Ben and the London Eye. The London Eye is almost 443 feet high and it is one of the world's tallest observation wheels. About 3.5 million people visit it each year to see the view from the top. Passengers can see for 24 miles in all directions.

Did you know?

◇ There are more tomatoes grown in Portugal than any other crop. Over 1 million tons of tomatoes are produced every year.

◇ The southern tip of Spain is only 8 miles from Africa at its closest point.

◇ Belgium is famous for making chocolate and produces over 192 tons of chocolates every year.

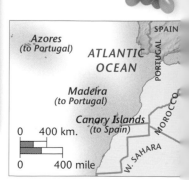

Grapes grow on plants called vines, and the areas where wine is produced are called vineyards.

SPAIN
Azores (to Portugal)
ATLANTIC OCEAN
PORTUGAL
Madeira (to Portugal)
Canary Islands (to Spain)
MOROCCO
0   400 km.
0   400 mile
W. SAHARA

Shetland
Islands

Orkney
Islands

Outer
Hebrides

Inverness

Aberdeen

SCOTLAND

Dundee

Glasgow · ★ Edinburgh

Ireland

NORTHERN
IRELAND

Belfast ★

UNITED
KINGDOM

Newcastle
upon Tyne

Galway

DUBLIN

IRELAND ★

Manchester

Leeds

Liverpool

Sheffield

ENGLAND

Limerick

Birmingham

Cork

WALES

Cardiff

LONDON ★

United Kingdom

Bristol

Thames

Plymouth

Southampton

English Channel

CHANNEL ISLANDS
(to U.K.)

Le Havre

Seine

Brest

Rennes

Orléans

Belgium

Netherlands

*North
Sea*

Groningen

NETHERLANDS

AMSTERDAM

THE
HAGUE

Utrecht

Rotterdam

Eindhoven

Ghent

Antwerp

Lille

★ BRUSSELS

BELGIUM

★ LUXEMBOURG

LUXEMBOURG

Amiens

Reims

Strasbourg

★ PARIS

GERMANY

Meuse

Rhine

Tulip fields

The Netherlands is famous for its flower bulbs and it produces 9 billion bulbs every year. In spring, the Dutch tulip fields near Amsterdam are ablaze with color. Visitors come from all around the world to see them.

Hedgehog

This small mammal lives in many parts of Europe. It has thousands of short spines over its back. If danger threatens it rolls itself into a prickly ball.

ATLANTIC OCEAN

N

Luxembourg

France

Bay of
Biscay

Nantes

Loire

FRANCE

Limoges

Clermont-
Ferrand

Dijon

SWITZERLAND

Mt. Blanc
15,782 ft ▲

Lyon

A
L
P
S

ITALY

Bordeaux

Dordogne

St-Étienne

Grenoble

Rhône

MASSIF
CENTRAL

Caronne

Toulouse

Montpellier

Nice

MONACO

Marseille

Monaco

A Coruña

Gijón

Santander

Oviedo

Bilbao

Vigo

Vitoria-Gasteiz

Ebro

PYRENEES

Perpignan

Corsica

Ajaccio

Viana do Castelo

Braga

Oporto

Duero

Valladolid

Zaragoza

ANDORRA

Lleida

Costa Brava

Barcelona

Mediterranean Sea

Eiffel Tower

This famous European landmark is in Paris, France. The Eiffel Tower is over 3,280 feet high, including the TV antenna. It is made almost entirely of wrought iron.

Spain

Coimbra

PORTUGAL

★ MADRID

SPAIN

Toledo

Majorca

Minorca

Palma

LISBON ★

Tagus

Mérida

Guadiana

Valencia

Ibiza

Balearic Islands

Portugal

Setúbal

Albacete

Alicante

Seville

Córdoba

Murcia

Guadalquivir

Faro

Granada

Málaga

Andorra

100   200 kilometers

Gibraltar (to U.K.)

100   200 miles

AFRICA

Central Europe
EUROPE

The central part of Europe stretches from the Baltic Sea in the north to the Mediterranean Sea in the south. Winters can be very cold in the north, but the weather gets warmer the further south you go. In Germany and Poland, land is used for mining, industry, and farming. People grow crops such as potatoes and barley, and many farmers keep pigs and goats. Farther south, especially in Italy, people grow olives, grapes, and citrus fruit. Many long rivers run through central Europe, including the Rhine and the Danube. People use these rivers for transporting their goods. A high mountain range called the Alps runs through France, Switzerland, Austria, and northern Italy.

Country File

Austria

Czech Republic

Germany

Italy

Liechtenstein

Malta

Poland

San Marino

Slovakia

Slovenia

Switzerland

Vatican City

Alps
This range of mountains is mainly in France, Italy, Switzerland, and Austria and is over 745 miles long. Many people visit the Alps to climb, walk, and ski. They are the source of several major European rivers, such as the Rhine, Rhone, and Po.

Did you know?
◇ Brown coal (lignite), is central Europe's main fuel and is one of Poland's main exports. It contains lots of sulphur, and burning it to make electricity adds to air pollution and acid rain.

◇ There are lots of different car manufacturers in Italy. Italy has one of the highest number of cars per person in the world.

Lamborghini cars are some of the fastest, most expensive sports cars in the world.

Did you know?
◇ Germany produces enough of the major food products, such as grains, sugar, oils, milk, and meat, for its whole population.

Vatican City
The Vatican City is in Rome, Italy. This is the smallest country in the world and it takes up an area of only 526,236 square yards. It contains St. Peter's Basilica and the Apostolic Palace, where the pope lives.

Tomatoes and basil are important ingredients in many Italian dishes, including pizza.

Alpine ibex
The ibex is a type of wild goat. It lives high up in the Alps and is sturdy and sure-footed. The ibex was hunted almost to extinction in the 19th century but now its numbers are growing.

National parks
There are many national parks in central Europe. This is Triglav National Park in Slovenia. It contains Triglav mountain, which is the highest peak in Slovenia. There are beech and spruce forests, and animals such as chamois and lynx live here.

Did you know?
◇ The highest peak in the Alps is Mont Blanc, on the border of Italy and France. It is 15,771 feet high.

◇ Pizza and pasta are Italian foods, but they are now enjoyed all over the world.

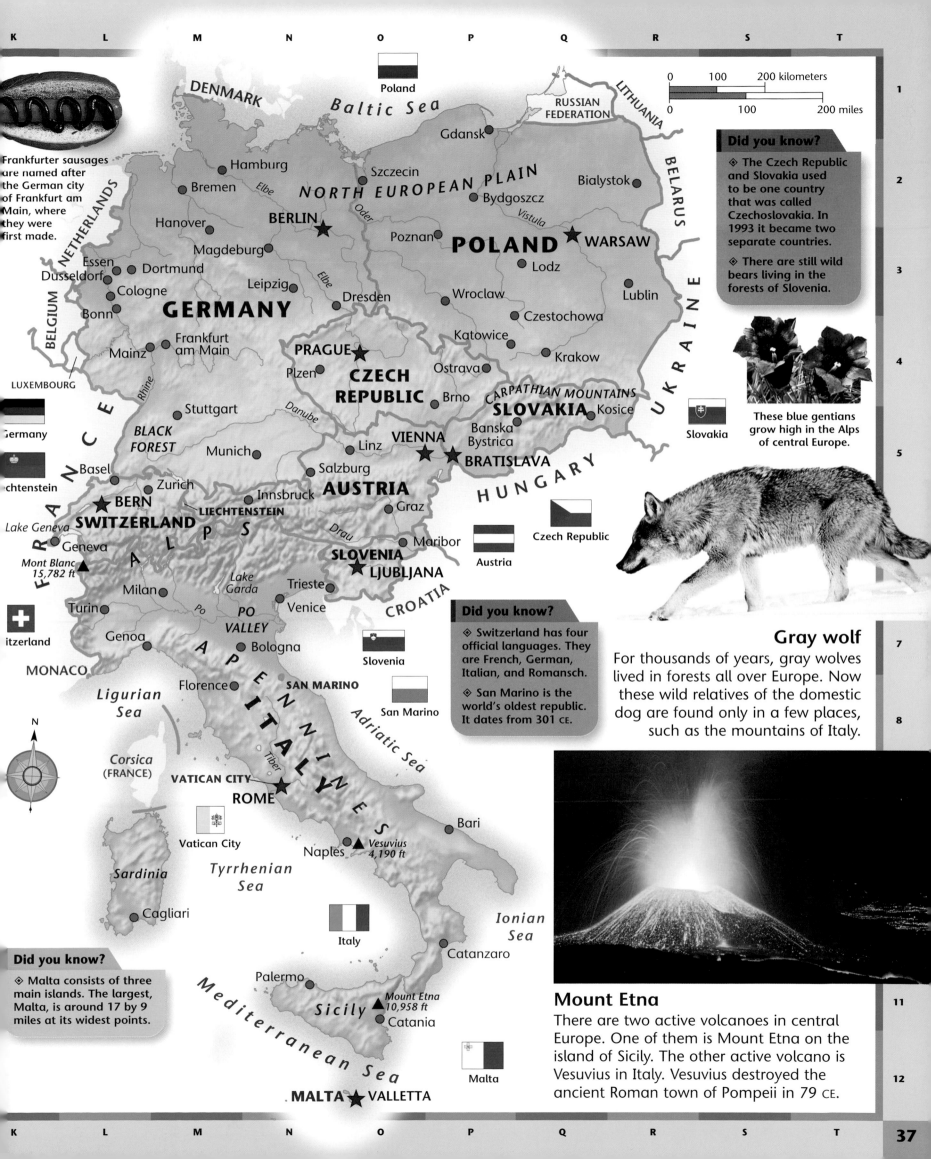

Frankfurter sausages are named after the German city of Frankfurt am Main, where they were first made.

DENMARK

Baltic Sea

NORTH EUROPEAN PLAIN

RUSSIAN FEDERATION

LITHUANIA

Gdansk

Hamburg

Bremen

Szczecin

Bialystok

BELARUS

Bydgoszcz

Poland

Elbe

Hanover

BERLIN

Oder

Poznan

POLAND

WARSAW

Magdeburg

Vistula

NETHERLANDS

Essen

Dortmund

Leipzig

Lodz

Dusseldorf

Cologne

Elbe

Dresden

Wroclaw

Lublin

BELGIUM

Bonn

GERMANY

Czestochowa

Mainz

Frankfurt am Main

PRAGUE

Katowice

Krakow

LUXEMBOURG

Rhine

Plzen

CZECH REPUBLIC

Ostrava

UKRAINE

Germany

Stuttgart

Danube

Brno

CARPATHIAN MOUNTAINS

SLOVAKIA

Kosice

BLACK FOREST

Munich

Linz

VIENNA

Banska Bystrica

Slovakia

chtenstein

Basel

Zurich

Salzburg

BRATISLAVA

Czech Republic

BERN

Innsbruck

AUSTRIA

HUNGARY

LIECHTENSTEIN

Graz

Austria

Lake Geneva

SWITZERLAND

Drau

Maribor

SLOVENIA

Mont Blanc 15,782 ft ▲

Geneva

LJUBLJANA

Milan

Lake Garda

Trieste

Slovenia

Po

PO VALLEY

Venice

itzerland

Turin

Genoa

Bologna

CROATIA

MONACO

Ligurian Sea

Florence

SAN MARINO

San Marino

N

Corsica (FRANCE)

VATICAN CITY

Tiber

ITALY

Adriatic Sea

ROME

Vatican City

Bari

Vesuvius 4,190 ft ▲

Naples

Sardinia

Tyrrhenian Sea

APENNINES

Italy

Ionian Sea

Cagliari

Catanzaro

Palermo

Mount Etna 10,958 ft ▲

Sicily

Catania

Mediterranean Sea

Malta

MALTA ★ VALLETTA

Did you know?

◈ The Czech Republic and Slovakia used to be one country that was called Czechoslovakia. In 1993 it became two separate countries.

◈ There are still wild bears living in the forests of Slovenia.

These blue gentians grow high in the Alps of central Europe.

Did you know?

◈ Switzerland has four official languages. They are French, German, Italian, and Romansch.

◈ San Marino is the world's oldest republic. It dates from 301 CE.

Gray wolf

For thousands of years, gray wolves lived in forests all over Europe. Now these wild relatives of the domestic dog are found only in a few places, such as the mountains of Italy.

Did you know?

◈ Malta consists of three main islands. The largest, Malta, is around 17 by 9 miles at its widest points.

Mount Etna

There are two active volcanoes in central Europe. One of them is Mount Etna on the island of Sicily. The other active volcano is Vesuvius in Italy. Vesuvius destroyed the ancient Roman town of Pompeii in 79 CE.

Southeast Europe

EUROPE

Much of this area is mountainous, although there are fertile, flat areas in the north and east. Farming is important in these countries and many crops, such as grapes, tobacco, roses, and wheat, are grown. In the north, the winters are very cold. Further south and around the coast, winters are milder and summers are hot and dry. During the past 30 years there have been many changes and wars in southeast Europe, caused by political, ethnic, and religious problems. In the 1990s, Ukraine, Belarus, and Moldova gained independence from the former Soviet Union. The former Yugoslavia split into the republics of Croatia, Serbia, Bosnia and Herzegovina, Macedonia, and Montenegro. After years of war, some areas are still recovering from their problems.

Country File

- Albania
- Belarus
- Bosnia and Herzegovina
- Bulgaria
- Croatia
- Greece
- Hungary
- Macedonia
- Moldova
- Montenegro
- Romania
- Serbia
- Ukraine

Most of the world's rose oil is produced in Bulgaria. Rose oil is used in luxury perfumes, soaps, and cosmetics and is more valuable than gold.

Did you know?

◈ The percentage of people who smoke cigarettes is higher in Romania than in any other European country.

◈ Some of the water from the springs in Budapest is over 194°F. It has to be mixed with cold water before it can be used.

Dubrovnik

The town of Dubrovnik in Croatia is encircled by almost 6,365 feet of city walls, which were built over 400 years ago. There are several towers and fortresses along the walls, making it one of the strongest fortifications in Europe.

Did you know?

◈ The huge Lake Prespa has an area of around 106 square miles. Most of it is in Macedonia, but some is in Albania and some in Greece. It is fed by underground streams and is linked by underground channels to Lake Ohrid. This even bigger lake, which is over 138 square miles, is shared by Macedonia and Albania.

Budapest

The Hungarian city of Budapest sits on a geological fault line. There are more than 120 springs in the city, where hot water rises naturally from the ground. People have built spas and baths over the hot springs for almost 2,000 years.

Wild boar

There are wild boar roaming freely throughout the forests of southeast Europe. These nocturnal animals forage for food from dusk until dawn. They live in groups called "sounders," containing about 20 animals. The groups are made up of three or four females and their young.

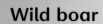

Olives have been grown in Greece for over 2,000 years, and olives and olive oil are major exports. Olives are also important ingredients in many dishes, including Greek salads.

Acropolis

Athens, the capital of Greece, is named after Athena, the goddess of war in Greek mythology. The Parthenon is Athena's chief temple. It was built in the 5th century BCE on the Acropolis hill above Athens. Acropolis means "edge of the city."

Ukraine

The rich dark soil of Ukraine is ideal for farming. Formerly part of the Soviet Union, Ukraine used to be known as "the bread basket of Russia." Today it exports large amounts of grain, vegetables, dairy produce, meat, and sunflower seeds.

Bosnia and Herzegovina

Hungary

Croatia

Serbia

Montenegro

Albania

Did you know?

◇ The European bison has been reintroduced to the Byelavyezhskaya forest in Belarus and Poland. It was extinct in the wild.

◇ The spotted Dalmatian dog gets its name from the Dalmatia region of Croatia.

Did you know?

◇ Ukraine relies heavily on Russia for its energy supplies, in particular oil and gas.

◇ One in four people in the Ukraine works in agriculture (farming) or forestry.

Belarus

Ukraine

Much of the soil in Moldova is rich and fertile. Many vegetables are grown there, but grapes and sunflowers are the most important crops.

Moldova

Romania

Bulgaria

Macedonia

Greece

Pine marten

These animals are related to weasels and are about the size of a domestic cat. They live in wooded areas all over Europe and spend a lot of their time in trees, where they build their dens. Pine martens feed mostly on small mammals, birds, frogs, insects, and carrion.

0   100   200 kilometers
0   100   200 miles

Map labels

LITHUANIA
LATVIA
RUSSIAN FEDERATION
Vitsyebsk
BELARUS
MINSK
Mahilyow
Hrodna
Babruysk
Homyel'
Brest
Dnieper
Pripet
Pripet Marshes
Chernihiv
Chernobyl'
Luts'k
KIEV
Kharkiv
Donets
Zhytomyr
UKRAINE
Poltava
Luhans'k
L'viv
Cherkasy
Dnipropetrovs'k
POLAND
Ivano-Frankivs'k
Kirovohrad
Dnieper
Donets'k
CARPATHIAN MOUNTAINS
Chernivtsi
Dniester
Zaporizhzhya
SLOVAKIA
MOLDOVA
Southern Bug
Kryvvy Rih
Mariupol'
AUSTRIA
Miskolc
Nyiregyhaza
Iasi
CHISINAU
Mykolayiv
BLACK SEA LOWLAND
Sea of Azov
Gyor
Tisza
Debrecen
Prut
Tiraspol'
SLOVENIA
BUDAPEST
Cluj-Napoca
Bacau
Odesa
HUNGARY
Drava
Pecs
Szeged
Transylvania
ROMANIA
Crimea
Sea of Azov
ZAGREB
Rijeka
CROATIA
Osijek
Novi Sad
Timisoara
Brasov
Simferopol'
Sava
TRANSYLVANIAN ALPS
Galati
Banja Luka
Tuzla
Ploiesti
Braila
Black Sea
Zadar
BOSNIA & HERZEGOVINA
BELGRADE
BUCHAREST
Adriatic Sea
Dalmatia
SARAJEVO
SERBIA
Craiova
Danube
Split
Mostar
Montana
Ruse
Dubrovnik
Nis
BULGARIA
Constanta
MONTENEGRO
PRISTINA
BALKAN MOUNTAINS
Varna
PODGORICA
KOSOVO
SOFIA
Sliven
Burgas
Shkoder
RHODOPE
Plovdiv
(only partially recognized)
SKOPJE
Musala 9,596 ft
MOUNTAINS
Durres
MACEDONIA
Komotini
TIRANA
Lake Ohrid
Bitola
Kavala
TURKEY
ALBANIA
Lake Prespa
Salonica
Kerkyra
PINDOS MOUNTAINS
Larisa
Aegean Sea
Corfu
Arta
GREECE
Lesbos Sea
Ionian Sea
Lamia
ATHENS
TURKEY
Patra
Piraeus
Peloponnese
Cyclades
Dodecanese
Mediterranean Sea
Sea of Crete
Rhodes
Irakleio
Crete

N

Russian Federation

EUROPE AND ASIA

The Russian Federation is the largest country in the world and it stretches across two continents. The area to the west of the Ural Mountains is in Europe, and the area to the east is in Asia. Russia's climate varies massively, from Arctic weather in the north to mild weather in the south. More than three-quarters of the country is occupied by Siberia, but less than 30 percent of the population lives there because the region has such long, cold winters. Siberia contains huge deposits of oil and natural gas. Russia also has fertile farmland and rich mineral deposits. Its main exports are oil and oil products, natural gas, metals, wood, and wood products. Most of the people there are Russians, but there are more than 120 other ethnic groups with many different religions, languages, and cultures.

Country File

Russian Federation

Russian Federation

St. Basil's Cathedral

St. Basil's in Moscow is one of the most famous buildings in the world. It was built in Red Square by Tsar Ivan IV "the Terrible" and was finished in 1560, after five years of building. It is actually eight separate churches, joined together with a central tower.

Did you know?

◈ Lake Baikal is the deepest lake in the world, at over one mile deep. It is also the oldest freshwater lake.

◈ Russia has two great classical ballet companies, called the Bolshoi and Mariinsky (formerly called the Kirov), which are both famous in many parts of the world.

Siberian tiger

The Siberian tiger is in danger of extinction. Its habitat is being destroyed and it is hunted for its body parts, which are used in traditional Chinese medicine. There are only about 500 left in the wild.

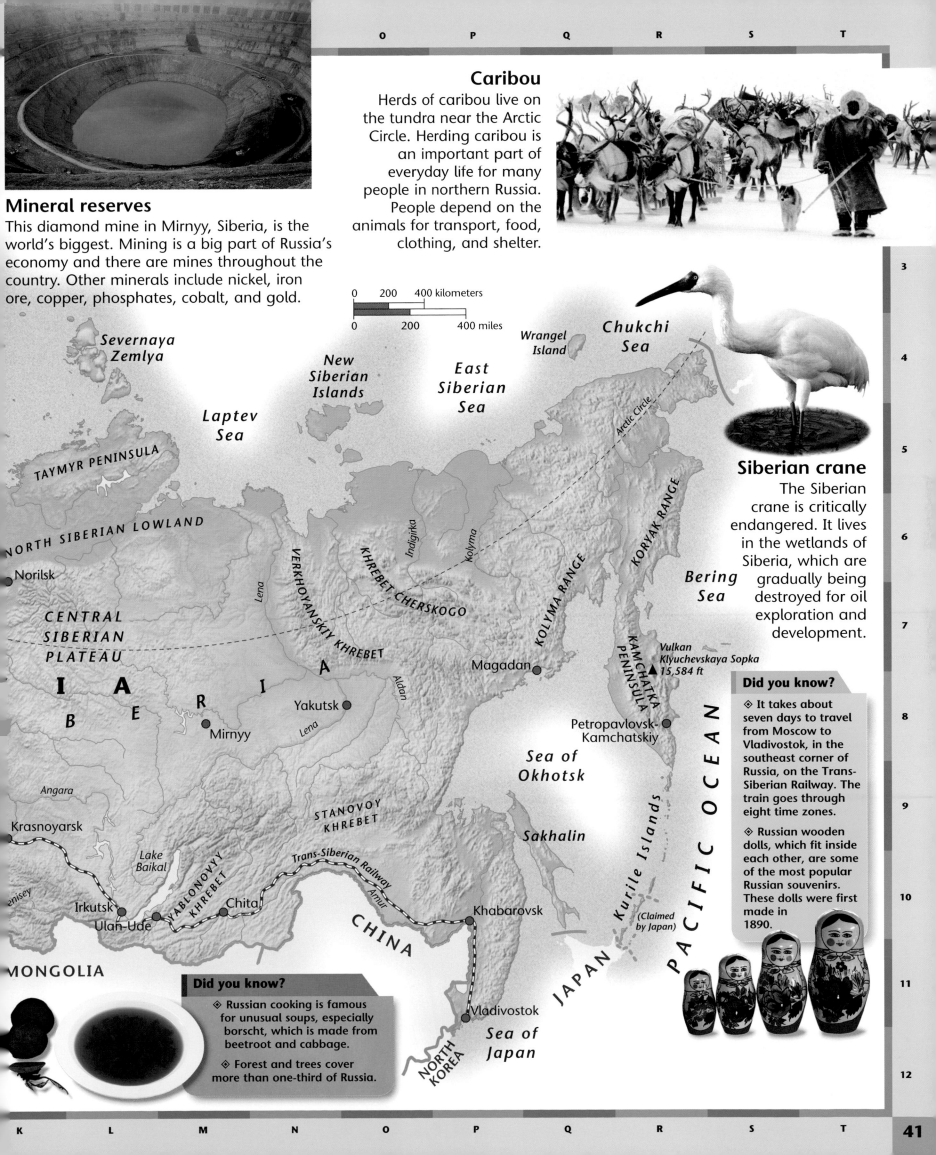

Caribou

Herds of caribou live on the tundra near the Arctic Circle. Herding caribou is an important part of everyday life for many people in northern Russia. People depend on the animals for transport, food, clothing, and shelter.

Mineral reserves

This diamond mine in Mirnyy, Siberia, is the world's biggest. Mining is a big part of Russia's economy and there are mines throughout the country. Other minerals include nickel, iron ore, copper, phosphates, cobalt, and gold.

0   200   400 kilometers

0   200   400 miles

Severnaya Zemlya

New Siberian Islands

East Siberian Sea

Wrangel Island

Chukchi Sea

Laptev Sea

TAYMYR PENINSULA

Arctic Circle

Siberian crane

The Siberian crane is critically endangered. It lives in the wetlands of Siberia, which are gradually being destroyed for oil exploration and development.

NORTH SIBERIAN LOWLAND

Norilsk

CENTRAL SIBERIAN PLATEAU

Lena

VERKHOYANSKIY KHREBET

KHREBET CHERSKOGO

Indigirka

Kolyma

KOLYMA RANGE

KORYAK RANGE

Bering Sea

S I B E R I A

Magadan

Aldan

Yakutsk

Mirnyy

Lena

KAMCHATKA PENINSULA

Vulkan Klyuchevskaya Sopka 15,584 ft

Petropavlovsk-Kamchatskiy

Sea of Okhotsk

Did you know?

◈ It takes about seven days to travel from Moscow to Vladivostok, in the southeast corner of Russia, on the Trans-Siberian Railway. The train goes through eight time zones.

◈ Russian wooden dolls, which fit inside each other, are some of the most popular Russian souvenirs. These dolls were first made in 1890.

Angara

STANOVOY KHREBET

Sakhalin

Krasnoyarsk

Lake Baikal

YABLONOVYY KHREBET

Trans-Siberian Railway

Amur

Kurile Islands

(Claimed by Japan)

P A C I F I C   O C E A N

Enisey

Irkutsk

Chita

Khabarovsk

Ulan-Ude

CHINA

JAPAN

MONGOLIA

Did you know?

◈ Russian cooking is famous for unusual soups, especially borscht, which is made from beetroot and cabbage.

◈ Forest and trees cover more than one-third of Russia.

Vladivostok

NORTH KOREA

Sea of Japan

3
4
5
6
7
8
9
10
11
12

Southwest Asia
ASIA

Cyprus

BULGARIA

Istanb

Bur

Izmir

Denizli

TURKISH REPUBLIC
NORTHERN CYP
(recognized only by Tur

Syria

Me

Lebanon

Country File

Armenia

Azerbaijan

Bahrain

Cyprus

Georgia

Iran

Iraq

Israel

Jordan

Kuwait

Lebanon

Oman

Qatar

Saudi Arabia

Syria

Turkey

United Arab Emirates

Yemen

Almost all of Southwest Asia is desert. Temperatures can soar to over 86°F in the summer and very little rain falls. Although the weather is hot and dry, people have lived here, in cities and towns, for over 7,000 years. Three of the world's most important religions started here: Christianity, Islam, and Judaism. This area has suffered wars for many thousands of years and the conflicts still continue. Most of the wars are about land ownership or disagreements about religion. The biggest source of income for many of these countries is from oil and gas. Oil has made some countries, such as the Arab states, very rich. Tourism is an important industry in several countries, including Turkey and Israel. Turkey and Iran are famous for carpets, which are exported around the world.

Mecca
The Ka'bah, a shrine inside the Sacred Mosque in Mecca in Saudi Arabia, is regarded by Muslims as the most sacred place on Earth. All able-bodied Muslims who can afford to are meant to make a pilgrimage there at least once in their lifetime.

Eggplants, apricots, pistachios, and walnuts are important crops in this area.

Petra
The ancient city of Petra in Jordan lies deep inside a desert gorge. Most of the buildings were carved out of solid rock. Once, this ruined city was the capital of an Arab kingdom. Now it is a popular tourist attraction.

Did you know?

◇ The lowest land on Earth that is not covered by ice is next to the Dead Sea. The shores of this lake are over 1,312 feet below sea level.

◇ Turkey is one of the few countries in the world that produces enough food for all its people. Half of the land in Turkey is used for agriculture (farming).

Dubai
The Burj al-Arab hotel in Dubai in the United Arab Emirates was the tallest hotel in the world when it opened in 1999. It is 1,053 feet high and has a helicopter pad on the 28th floor. The hotel stands on an artificial island and it was designed to look like a big sail.

Arabian oryx
The Arabian oryx was hunted to extinction in the wild. Then, after a worldwide breeding program in zoos, it was re-introduced into the wild in Oman. Today there are herds of oryx roaming freely in several countries.

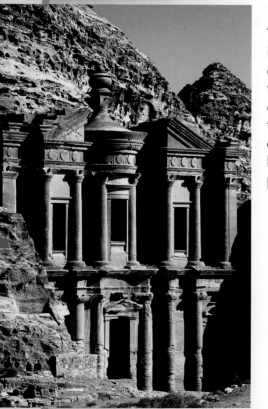

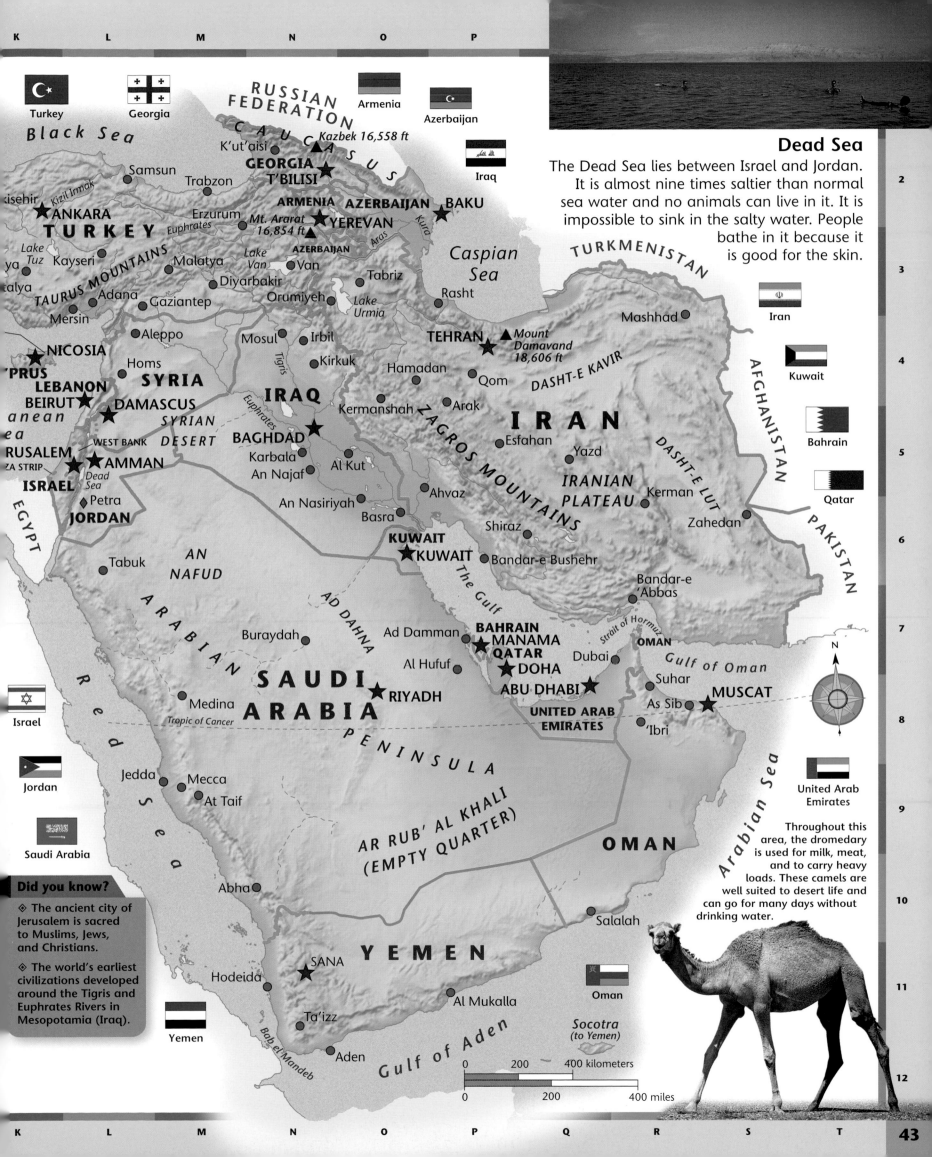

Turkey

Georgia

Armenia

Azerbaijan

Iraq

RUSSIAN FEDERATION

Black Sea

C A U C A S U S

Kazbek 16,558 ft ▲

K'ut'aisi

GEORGIA
T'BILISI ★

Samsun

Trabzon

...isehir

Kizil Irmak

★ **ANKARA**

T U R K E Y

Erzurum

Euphrates

ARMENIA

Mt. Ararat
16,854 ft ▲

AZERBAIJAN

★ **YEREVAN**

★ **BAKU**

AZERBAIJAN

Aras

Kura

*Caspian
Sea*

T U R K M E N I S T A N

*Lake
Tuz*

Kayseri

Malatya

Diyarbakir

*Lake
Van*

Van

Tabriz

Rasht

Mashhad

...ya

...alya

T A U R U S   M O U N T A I N S

Adana

Gaziantep

Orumiyeh

*Lake
Urmia*

Mersin

Aleppo

Mosul

Irbil

TEHRAN ★

▲ *Mount
Damavand
18,606 ft*

★ **NICOSIA**

Homs

S Y R I A

Tigris

Kirkuk

Hamadan

Qom

DASHT-E KAVIR

...PRUS

LEBANON

IRAQ

Kermanshah

Arak

I R A N

Esfahan

Yazd

BEIRUT ★

★ **DAMASCUS**

SYRIAN

BAGHDAD ★

Euphrates

...anean
...ea

RUSALEM

WEST BANK

DESERT

Karbala

An Najaf

Al Kut

Ahvaz

Z A G R O S   M O U N T A I N S

Shiraz

Kerman

**IRANIAN
PLATEAU**

DASHT-E LUT

Zahedan

A F G H A N I S T A N

P A K I S T A N

...ZA STRIP

★ **AMMAN**

*Dead
Sea*

ISRAEL

◆ Petra

JORDAN

An Nasiriyah

Basra

E G Y P T

Tabuk

**A N
N A F U D**

KUWAIT
★ **KUWAIT**

Bandar-e Bushehr

The Gulf

Bandar-e
'Abbas

A R A B I A N

A D   D A H N A

Buraydah

Ad Damman

**BAHRAIN
MANAMA**

Strait of Hormuz

OMAN

Gulf of Oman

N

Al Hufuf

QATAR
★ **DOHA**

Dubai

Suhar

MUSCAT ★

Red

S A U D I

★ **RIYADH**

ABU DHABI ★

**UNITED ARAB
EMIRATES**

As Sib ●★

'Ibri

Medina

A R A B I A

Tropic of Cancer

P E N I N S U L A

Iran

Kuwait

Bahrain

Qatar

Israel

Jordan

Saudi Arabia

United Arab
Emirates

Sea

Jedda

Mecca

At Taif

**AR RUB' AL KHALI
(EMPTY QUARTER)**

O M A N

Arabian Sea

Abha

Salalah

Y E M E N

★ **SANA**

Hodeida

Al Mukalla

Oman

Yemen

Ta'izz

*Socotra
(to Yemen)*

Bab el Mandeb

Aden

Gulf of Aden

Dead Sea

The Dead Sea lies between Israel and Jordan. It is almost nine times saltier than normal sea water and no animals can live in it. It is impossible to sink in the salty water. People bathe in it because it is good for the skin.

Throughout this area, the dromedary is used for milk, meat, and to carry heavy loads. These camels are well suited to desert life and can go for many days without drinking water.

Did you know?

◇ The ancient city of Jerusalem is sacred to Muslims, Jews, and Christians.

◇ The world's earliest civilizations developed around the Tigris and Euphrates Rivers in Mesopotamia (Iraq).

0   200   400 kilometers

0   200   400 miles

2
3
4
5
6
7
8
9
10
11
12

Central Asia

ASIA

The Pamirs, in the southeast of this region, form the second highest mountain range in the world (the Himalayas are the highest). Mountains also cover most of Kyrgyzstan and Tajikistan and much of Afghanistan. Kazakhstan has open grasslands, and farther south in Uzbekistan and Turkmenistan there is a lot of sandy desert. Central Asia is land-locked, which means that it is cut off from the sea, although it has a huge inland lake called the Caspian Sea. This area gets very little rain and winters and summers have extreme temperatures. There are few large cities and most people live in rural areas. Most of the farming is around the fertile river valleys at the base of the mountains and in Kazakhstan. The main crops include cotton, peaches, melons, and apricots. Central Asia has large deposits of oil, coal, and natural gas, and minerals such as iron and copper. Industries are mostly traditional ones, and some areas specialize in making carpets and leather goods.

Country File

Afghanistan

Kazakhstan

Kyrgyzstan

Tajikistan

Turkmenistan

Uzbekistan

Ural'sk

RUSSIAN FEDERATION

Caspian Depression

Atyrau

Aktau

Caspian Sea

Turkmenbasy

Balkanabat

Aral Sea

The Aral Sea once covered an area of 26,255 square miles. But since 1960, it has shrunk to a quarter of its size because water from rivers that flow into the lake is being diverted to use for irrigation. Old ships that used to float on the lake are now sitting on dry land.

Samarqand

One of the oldest cities in Central Asia is Samarqand, which contains some of the finest buildings in this area. They include several Islamic schools called madrasahs. Shirdar madrasah, shown here, was built in the early 1600s. It is decorated with millions of tiles.

Snow leopard

The snow leopard lives high in the mountains of Central Asia. This big cat has very thick fur, which can be almost four inches long in places.

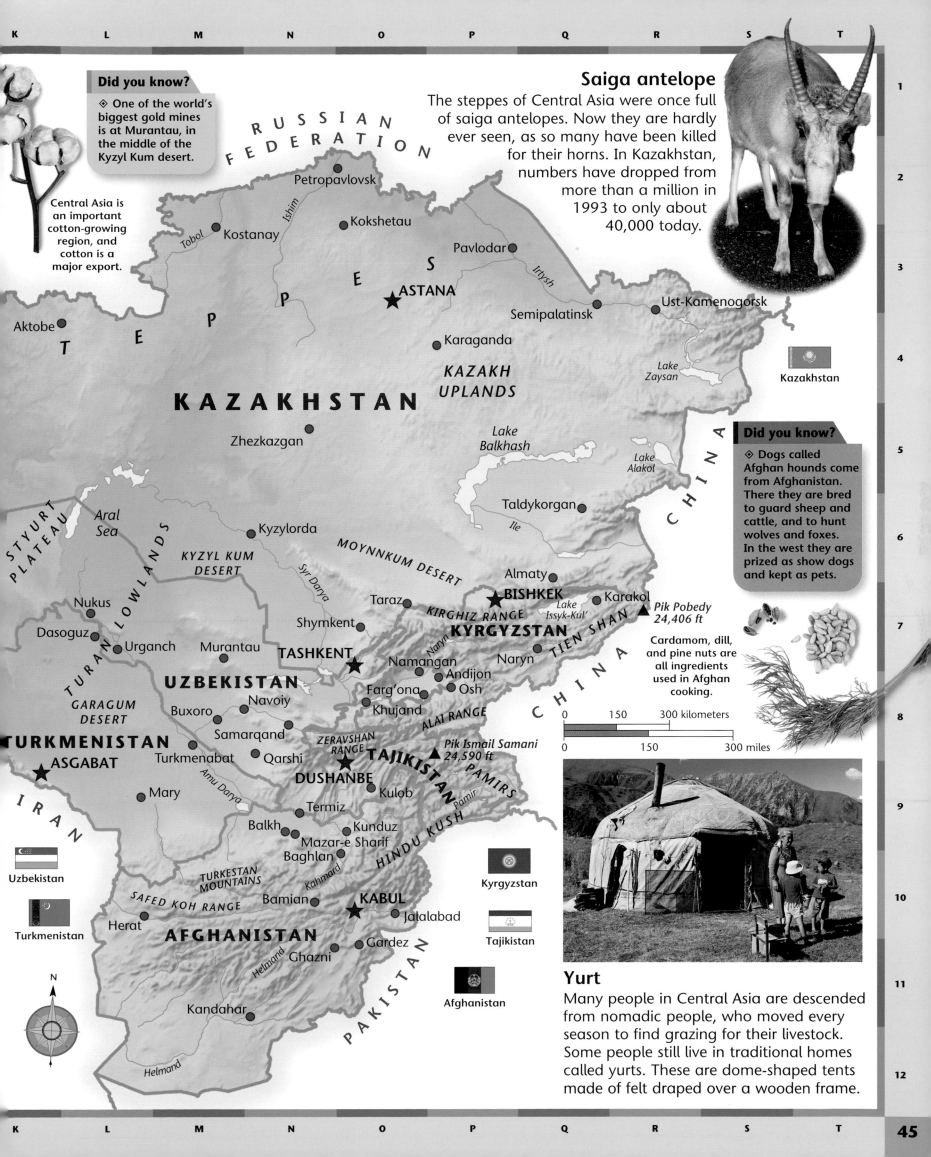

Did you know?

◈ One of the world's biggest gold mines is at Murantau, in the middle of the Kyzyl Kum desert.

Central Asia is an important cotton-growing region, and cotton is a major export.

Saiga antelope

The steppes of Central Asia were once full of saiga antelopes. Now they are hardly ever seen, as so many have been killed for their horns. In Kazakhstan, numbers have dropped from more than a million in 1993 to only about 40,000 today.

RUSSIAN FEDERATION

Petropavlovsk

Kokshetau

Tobol

Ishim

Kostanay

Pavlodar

Irtysh

ASTANA

Semipalatinsk

Ust-Kamenogorsk

Aktobe

Karaganda

Kazakhstan

KAZAKH UPLANDS

Lake Zaysan

KAZAKHSTAN

Zhezkazgan

Lake Balkhash

Lake Alakol

CHINA

Did you know?

◈ Dogs called Afghan hounds come from Afghanistan. There they are bred to guard sheep and cattle, and to hunt wolves and foxes. In the west they are prized as show dogs and kept as pets.

Aral Sea

Taldykorgan

Ile

STYURT PLATEAU

Kyzylorda

KYZYL KUM DESERT

Syr Darya

MOYNNKUM DESERT

Almaty

Nukus

TURAN LOWLANDS

Taraz

BISHKEK

Lake Issyk-Kul'

Karakol

Pik Pobedy 24,406 ft

Dasoguz

Shymkent

KIRGHIZ RANGE

KYRGYZSTAN

TIEN SHAN

Cardamom, dill, and pine nuts are all ingredients used in Afghan cooking.

Urganch

Murantau

Namangan

Naryn

Naryn

TASHKENT

Andijon

UZBEKISTAN

Farg'ona

Osh

Navoiy

Khujand

CHINA

GARAGUM DESERT

Buxoro

ALAI RANGE

0   150   300 kilometers

Samarqand

ZERAVSHAN RANGE

Pik Ismail Samani 24,590 ft

0   150   300 miles

TURKMENISTAN

Qarshi

TAJIKISTAN

PAMIRS

ASGABAT

Turkmenabat

DUSHANBE

Pamir

Mary

Amu Darya

Kulob

Termiz

Balkh

Kunduz

Uzbekistan

Mazar-e Sharif

HINDU KUSH

Baghlan

IRAN

TURKESTAN MOUNTAINS

Kahmard

Kyrgyzstan

Turkmenistan

SAFED KOH RANGE

Bamian

KABUL

Helmand

Jalalabad

Tajikistan

Herat

AFGHANISTAN

Gardez

Ghazni

N

PAKISTAN

Afghanistan

Yurt

Many people in Central Asia are descended from nomadic people, who moved every season to find grazing for their livestock. Some people still live in traditional homes called yurts. These are dome-shaped tents made of felt draped over a wooden frame.

Kandahar

Helmand

South Asia

ASIA

This area is also called the Indian subcontinent. South Asia is separated from the rest of Asia by the towering peaks of the Himalayas. The tops of these mountains are always covered in snow. In the south there are lush tropical rain forests, and in the west are huge areas of desert. India has a typical monsoon climate. From March to June it is hot and dry. The wet season is from June to September, when large amounts of rain fall, often causing floods. October to February is cool and dry. Over one-fifth of the world's population lives in this area. After centuries of invasion and occupation, people have a rich variety of cultures and religions and thousands of languages are spoken. Nearly two-thirds of the population work in agriculture, although most farmers grow only enough for their family. Rice grows in the wetter areas of the east and west, and millet and corn grow on higher areas inland. Tea is an important crop, especially in southwest India and Sri Lanka.

Country File

- Bangladesh
- Bhutan
- India
- Maldives
- Nepal
- Pakistan
- Sri Lanka

The population of India is the second biggest in the world (China has the largest population). There are now almost 1,190 million people living in India.

Pakistan

IRAN

CENTRAL MA RANGE

Did you know?

◈ Bangladesh is one of the most densely populated countries in the world and its population is one of the poorest. Most people survive by growing their own food.

◈ There are over 270 species of snake in India, including about 50 venomous ones, such as this king cobra.

A cobra rears up and spreads its hood when it is alarmed.

Bollywood

Film making in India is a huge industry and it is known as "Bollywood." The films often contain spectacular song-and-dance routines, with expert fight scenes and beautiful heroes and heroines. Bollywood is based in the city of Mumbai, which used to be called Bombay.

Did you know?

◈ Over 200 people have died trying to climb Mt. Everest, and every year this number is rising.

◈ The River Ganges is sacred to people who follow the Hindu religion and it is worshipped as a goddess.

◈ About 800 films are made every year in Bollywood.

Taj Mahal

The Mughal emperor Shah Jahan built the beautiful Taj Mahal in Agra, India, in memory of his favorite wife, Mumtaz Mahal. It took 22 years to build and was finished in 1648. The Taj Mahal consists of four buildings, one of which is a tomb containing the bodies of Shah Jahan and his wife.

Tea plantations

Sri Lanka and parts of India have the ideal climate for tea growing. Only the youngest tea leaves are picked. These are then wilted, oxidized, rolled, and dried to produce the tea that we use to make the popular drink.

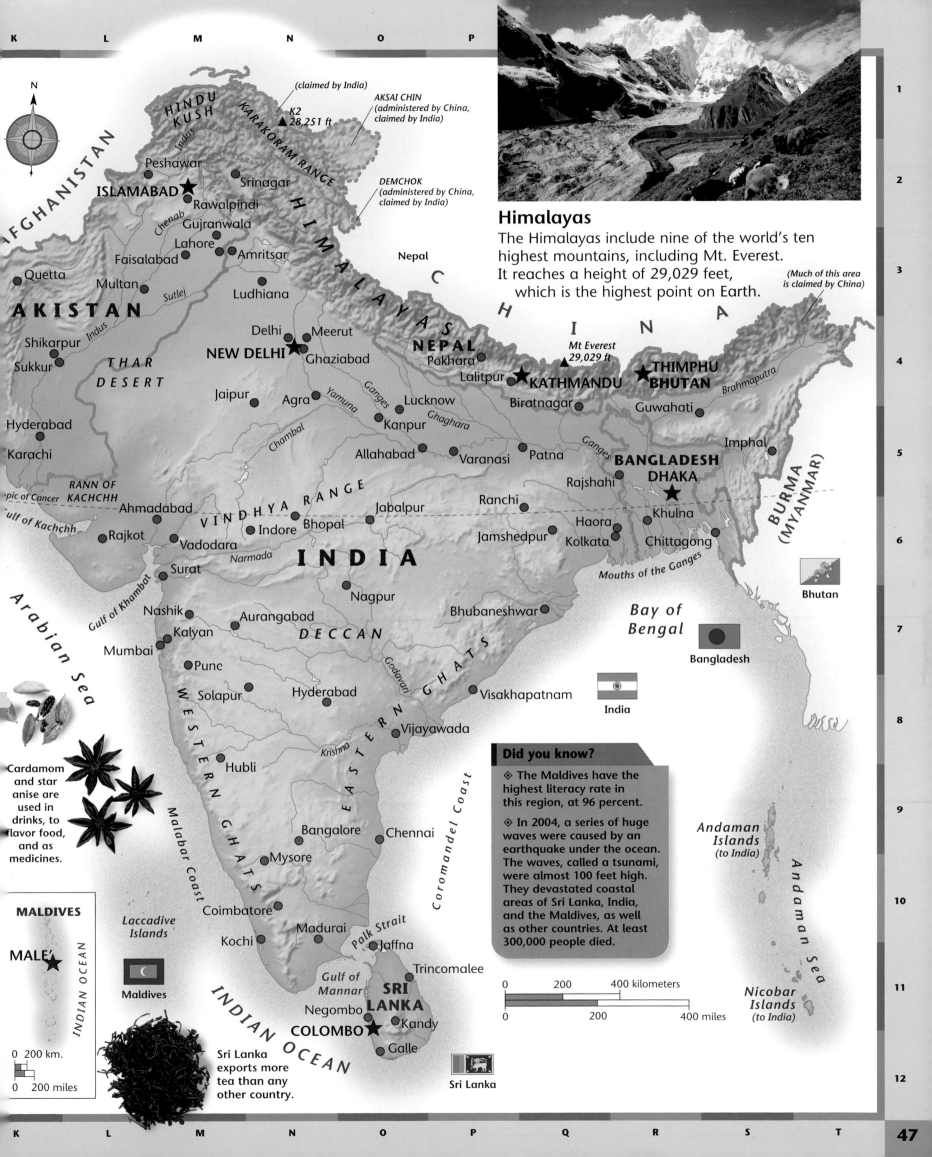

N

AFGHANISTAN

HINDU KUSH

Indus

KARAKORAM RANGE

(claimed by India)

K2
▲ 28,251 ft

AKSAI CHIN
(administered by China,
claimed by India)

DEMCHOK
(administered by China,
claimed by India)

Peshawar

ISLAMABAD ★

Srinagar

Rawalpindi

Chenab

Gujranwala

Lahore

Faisalabad

Amritsar

Nepal

HIMALAYAS

C   H   I   N   A

Himalayas

The Himalayas include nine of the world's ten highest mountains, including Mt. Everest. It reaches a height of 29,029 feet, which is the highest point on Earth.

(Much of this area is claimed by China)

Quetta

Multan

Sutlej

Ludhiana

AKISTAN

Shikarpur

Sukkur

Indus

THAR DESERT

Delhi

Meerut

NEW DELHI ★

Ghaziabad

NEPAL

Pokhara

Lalitpur

★ **KATHMANDU**

★ **THIMPHU**
BHUTAN

Mt Everest
29,029 ft ▲

Jaipur

Agra

Yamuna

Ganges

Lucknow

Ghaghara

Biratnagar

Guwahati

Brahmaputra

Imphal

Hyderabad

Kanpur

Chambal

Karachi

Allahabad

Varanasi

Patna

Ganges

BANGLADESH
DHAKA ★

RANN OF KACHCHH

Tropic of Cancer

Rajshahi

Ahmadabad

VINDHYA RANGE

Jabalpur

Ranchi

Khulna

Gulf of Kachchh

Indore

Bhopal

Haora

Kolkata

Chittagong

BURMA
(MYANMAR)

Rajkot

Vadodara

Narmada

INDIA

Jamshedpur

Mouths of the Ganges

Surat

Gulf of Khambat

Nagpur

Bhubaneshwar

Bay of Bengal

Bhutan

Nashik

Aurangabad

DECCAN

Kalyan

Mumbai

Pune

Hyderabad

Godavari

Visakhapatnam

Bangladesh

India

Arabian Sea

Solapur

WESTERN GHATS

EASTERN GHATS

Vijayawada

Krishna

Cardamom and star anise are used in drinks, to flavor food, and as medicines.

Hubli

Coromandel Coast

Did you know?

◇ The Maldives have the highest literacy rate in this region, at 96 percent.

◇ In 2004, a series of huge waves were caused by an earthquake under the ocean. The waves, called a tsunami, were almost 100 feet high. They devastated coastal areas of Sri Lanka, India, and the Maldives, as well as other countries. At least 300,000 people died.

Andaman Islands
(to India)

Bangalore

Chennai

Mysore

Andaman Sea

MALDIVES

Laccadive Islands

Coimbatore

Madurai

Palk Strait

Kochi

Jaffna

Trincomalee

Gulf of Mannar

SRI LANKA

| 0 | 200 | 400 kilometers |
| 0 | 200 | 400 miles |

Nicobar Islands
(to India)

MALE' ★

INDIAN OCEAN

Maldives

Negombo

COLOMBO ★

Kandy

Galle

INDIAN OCEAN

Malabar Coast

0 200 km.

0 200 miles

Sri Lanka exports more tea than any other country.

Sri Lanka

East Asia

ASIA

A large part of East Asia has a landscape of high mountains, desert, or steppe land. Some areas are remote, with long distances between towns, and the climate is extreme. In the southeast the land changes from mountains to wide river valleys and open plains. To the east is Japan, which has a rugged, mountainous landscape. Japan is one of the richest nations in the world. It does not have many natural resources, so it imports them. Japan is well known for making advanced electronic equipment. It is also a world leader in vehicle manufacturing. China and South Korea now have strong economies.

Country File

China

Japan

Mongolia

North Korea

South Korea

Taiwan

Did you know?

◇ Today more people live in Tokyo, which is the capital of Japan, than any other city in the world.

◇ Only about 15% of the land in Japan is suitable for farming, but Japan grows enough rice to feed its population.

KAZAKHSTAN

ALTAI MOUNTAINS

DZUNGARIAN BASIN

KYRGYZSTAN

TIEN SHAN

● Urumqi

TAJIKISTAN

TARIM BASIN

PAKISTAN

(Claimed by India)

TAKLA MAKAN DESERT

▲ K2 28,251 ft

KUNLUN MOUNTAINS   ALTUN SHAN   QILIAN SH

QAIDAM BASIN

INDIA

(Administered by China, claimed by India)

(Administered by China, claimed by India)

PLATEAU OF TIBET

C

Salween

H I M A L A Y A S

NEPAL

T i b e t

Brahmaputra   ● Lhasa

China

Mt. Everest 29,029 ft

BHUTAN   INDIA

Great Wall of China

One of the largest and longest structures on Earth is the Great Wall of China. It starts east of Bejing, near the Chinese coast and stretches inland, across northern China, for over 3,976 miles. This huge wall was started in 220 BCE and took 10 years to build. It was made to keep out invaders from the north, such as the Mongols.

Did you know?

◇ The official language of China is Mandarin, and more people speak this than any other language in the world.

◇ More than one-fifth of the world's population live in China. Most live in the southeast.

◇ In some areas of Mongolia, the temperature drops to -74.2°F, which is as cold as the Arctic.

Traditional herbal medicine, such as these wolf berries, has been used in China for over 4,500 years.

Giant panda

These are among the most endangered animals in the world. There are only around 1,600 left in the wild. Pandas are carnivores (meat eaters), but 99 percent of their diet is bamboo. Pandas live in thick bamboo forests in central China and spend around 14 hours a day eating!

BURMA

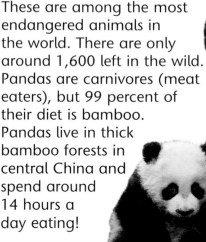

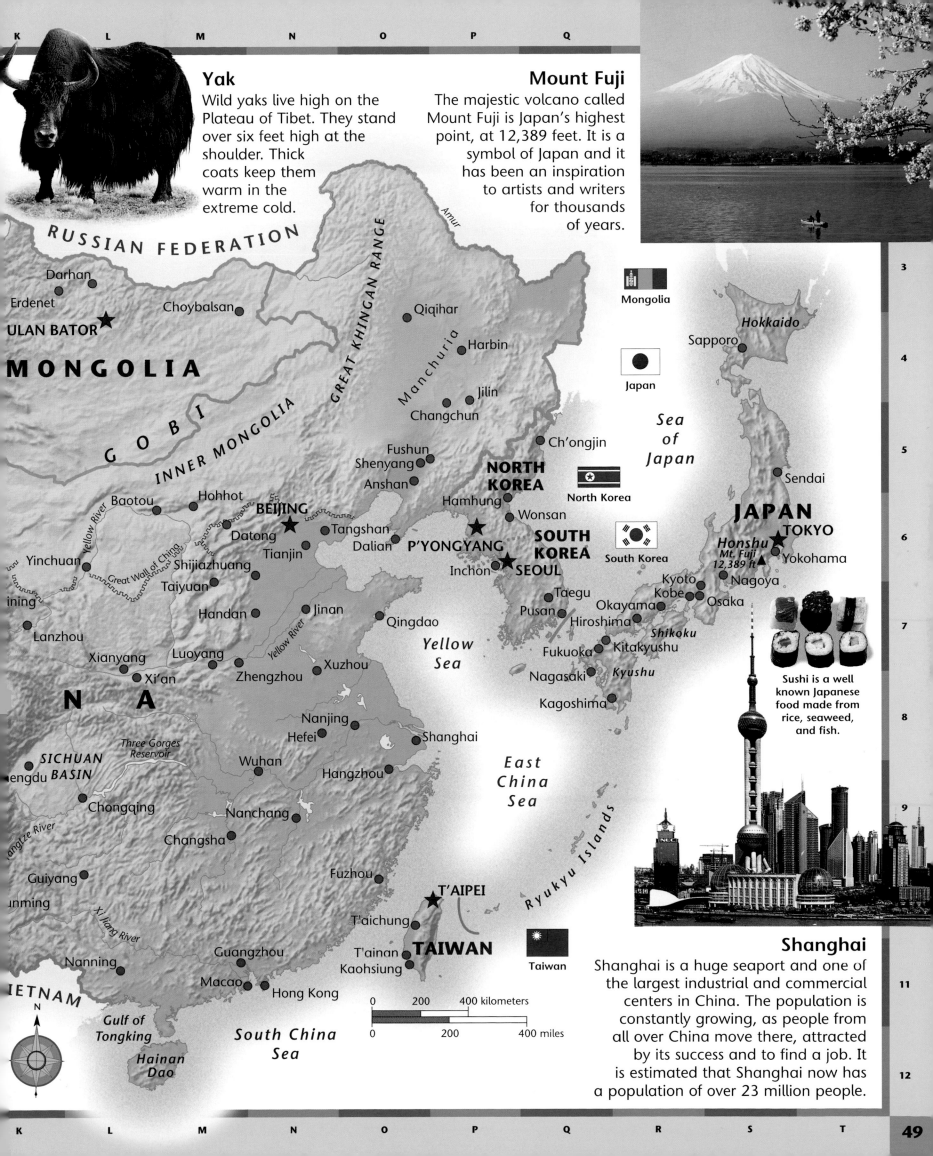

K L M N O P Q

Yak

Wild yaks live high on the Plateau of Tibet. They stand over six feet high at the shoulder. Thick coats keep them warm in the extreme cold.

Mount Fuji

The majestic volcano called Mount Fuji is Japan's highest point, at 12,389 feet. It is a symbol of Japan and it has been an inspiration to artists and writers for thousands of years.

RUSSIAN FEDERATION

Darhan
Erdenet
ULAN BATOR ★
Choybalsan

MONGOLIA

GOBI

INNER MONGOLIA

GREAT KHINGAN RANGE

Amur

Qiqihar

Manchuria

Harbin

Jilin

Changchun

Fushun
Shenyang
Anshan

Ch'ongjin

NORTH KOREA

Hamhung

Wonsan

P'YONGYANG ★

SOUTH KOREA

SEOUL ★
Inchon

Pusan
Taegu

Mongolia

Japan

North Korea

South Korea

Sea of Japan

Hokkaido

Sapporo

Sendai

JAPAN
TOKYO ★

Honshu
Mt. Fuji
12,389 ft ▲
Yokohama
Nagoya

Kyoto
Kobe
Osaka
Okayama
Hiroshima
Fukuoka
Kitakyushu
Shikoku
Nagasaki
Kyushu
Kagoshima

Baotou
Hohhot
Datong
BEIJING ★
Tangshan
Tianjin
Dalian
Shijiazhuang
Taiyuan
Yinchuan
Yellow River
Great Wall of China
ining
Lanzhou
Xianyang
Xi'an
Handan
Luoyang
Zhengzhou
Jinan
Yellow River
Xuzhou
Qingdao

Yellow Sea

Sushi is a well known Japanese food made from rice, seaweed, and fish.

N A

SICHUAN BASIN
engdu
Chongqing
Yangtze River
Nanchang
Changsha

Three Gorges Reservoir

Wuhan
Hangzhou
Nanjing
Hefei
Shanghai

East China Sea

Ryukyu Islands

Guiyang
nming
Xi Jiang River
Nanning
Guangzhou
Macao
Hong Kong

Fuzhou

T'AIPEI ★
T'aichung
T'ainan
Kaohsiung
TAIWAN

Taiwan

IETNAM
N

Gulf of Tongking

Hainan Dao

South China Sea

0 200 400 kilometers
0 200 400 miles

Shanghai

Shanghai is a huge seaport and one of the largest industrial and commercial centers in China. The population is constantly growing, as people from all over China move there, attracted by its success and to find a job. It is estimated that Shanghai now has a population of over 23 million people.

3
4
5
6
7
8
9
11
12

K L M N O P Q R S T

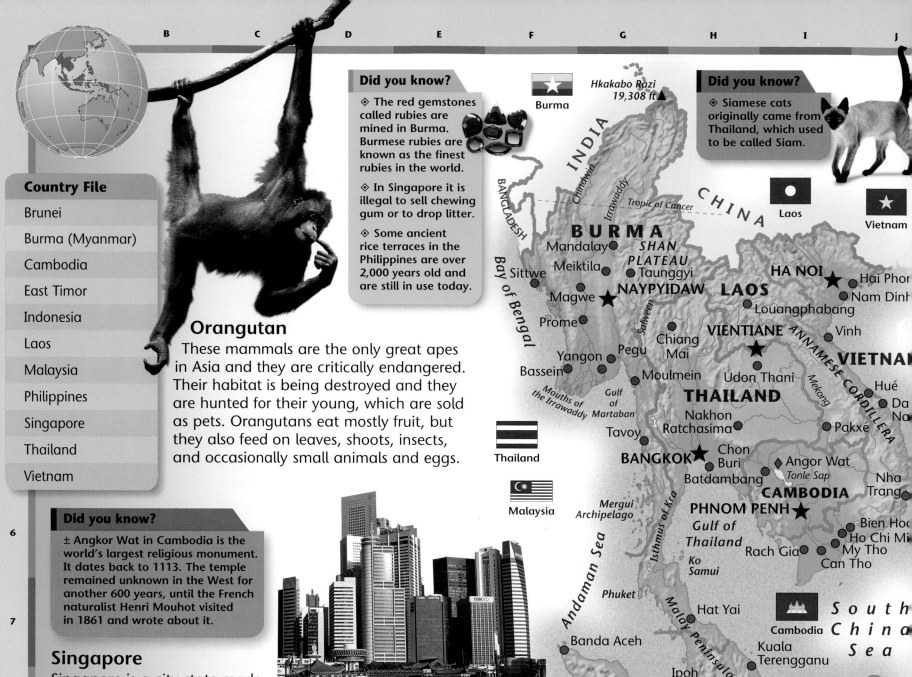

Country File

Brunei

Burma (Myanmar)

Cambodia

East Timor

Indonesia

Laos

Malaysia

Philippines

Singapore

Thailand

Vietnam

Did you know?

◈ The red gemstones called rubies are mined in Burma. Burmese rubies are known as the finest rubies in the world.

◈ In Singapore it is illegal to sell chewing gum or to drop litter.

◈ Some ancient rice terraces in the Philippines are over 2,000 years old and are still in use today.

Did you know?

◈ Siamese cats originally came from Thailand, which used to be called Siam.

Orangutan

These mammals are the only great apes in Asia and they are critically endangered. Their habitat is being destroyed and they are hunted for their young, which are sold as pets. Orangutans eat mostly fruit, but they also feed on leaves, shoots, insects, and occasionally small animals and eggs.

Did you know?

± Angkor Wat in Cambodia is the world's largest religious monument. It dates back to 1113. The temple remained unknown in the West for another 600 years, until the French naturalist Henri Mouhot visited in 1861 and wrote about it.

Singapore

Singapore is a city-state made up of a main island (Singapore Island) and 62 other islands. It is the biggest port in Southeast Asia, one of the world's main oil-refining centers and a world leader in ship building and repair. Singapore also has a thriving technology industry.

Did you know?

◈ After the rice harvest in Malaysia, farmers used to celebrate with kite-flying games. Today there is a big kite-flying festival in Malaysia every year.

Paddy fields

People grow rice throughout Southeast Asia. Rice needs plenty of water and heat so this area's climate is ideal. Rice fields are called paddy fields. Each field has a low wall so that it can be flooded with water. On steep slopes the paddy fields are built in terraces.

50

Southeast Asia

ASIA

Much of Southeast Asia is mountainous and covered in thick forest. This area has a tropical monsoon climate, when half of the year is wet and half is dry. Most of the people live in the river valleys, on the fertile plains of the mainland, or around the coasts of the islands. Some islands have no people living on them, but others, such as Java, have a big population. People in this area are from many different cultures. They follow lots of religions and speak hundreds of languages. The main industries are processing raw materials, such as oil, minerals, timber, and food. Recently, the manufacturing of electronic goods and also computers has increased.

Buddhism

One of the main religions in this area is Buddhism. Buddhist temples have steep roofs, pointed windows, and carved details. Like many Buddhist temples, this one is guarded by statues of lions at the entrance.

Lemongrass, lime, and coriander are important ingredients in Southeast Asian cooking.

Did you know?

◇ The sultan of Brunei has the largest palace in the world, built of marble, gold mosaics, and stained glass.

Komodo dragon

This is the largest lizard and it grows to almost 10 feet long. Komodo dragons live on the Lesser Sunda Islands. They are venomous and are fierce predators, eating anything that they can overpower. They slice through their victims with sharp, serrated teeth.

Unusual carved wooden masks like this one are worn by professional dancers in Indonesia.

Did you know?

◇ Indonesia is made up of over 17,500 islands. A group of islands like this is called an archipelago. Indonesia is one of the most volcanic parts of the world.

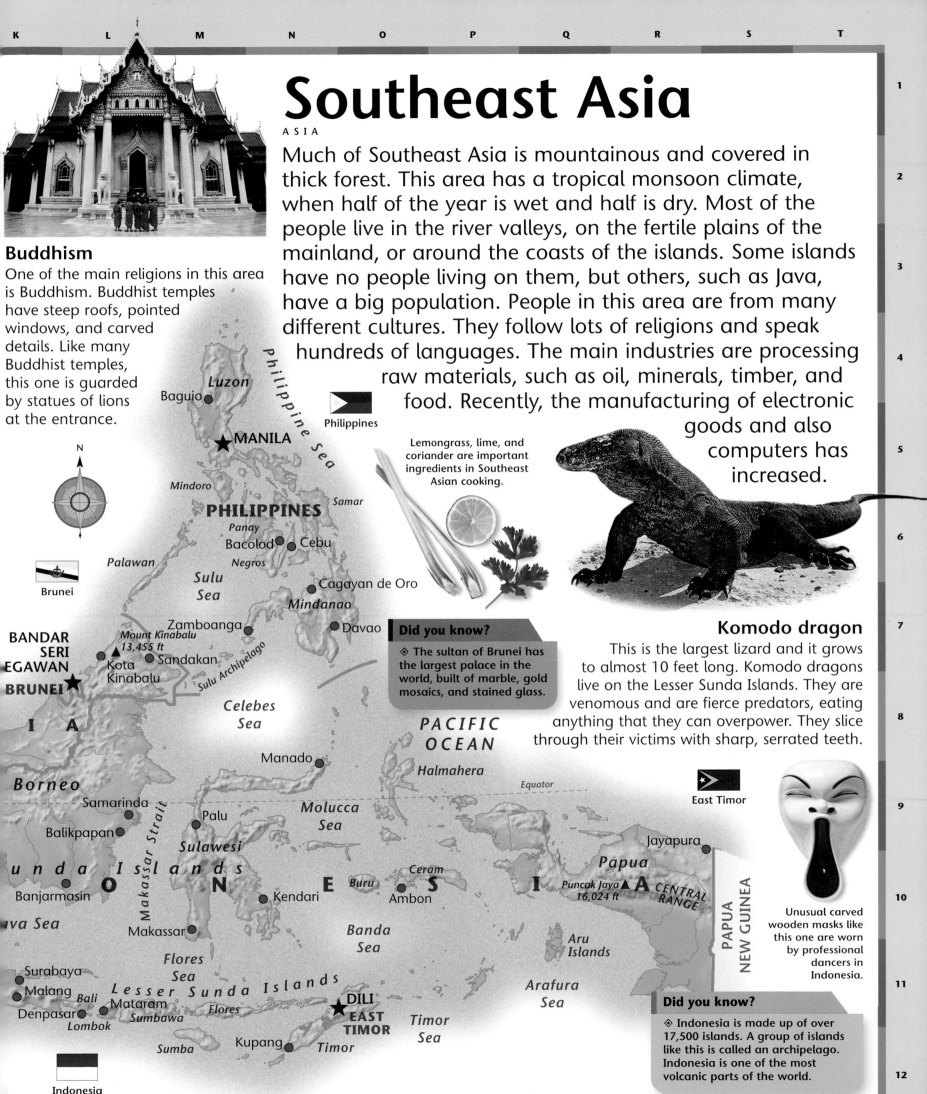

Philippines

Brunei

N

Luzon
Baguio
MANILA
Mindoro
Samar
PHILIPPINES
Panay
Bacolod
Cebu
Palawan
Negros
Sulu
Sea
Cagayan de Oro
Mindanao
Zamboanga
Davao
Mount Kinabalu
13,455 ft
Sandakan
BANDAR
SERI
EGAWAN
Kota
Kinabalu
Sulu Archipelago
BRUNEI
Celebes
Sea
PACIFIC
OCEAN
I   A
Manado
Halmahera
Borneo
Samarinda
Equator
East Timor
Palu
Molucca
Sea
Balikpapan
Jayapura
Sulawesi
u n d a   I s l a n d s
Ceram
Papua
Buru
Puncak Jaya
16,024 ft
CENTRAL
RANGE
Banjarmasin
Kendari
Ambon
PAPUA
NEW GUINEA
va Sea
Makassar
Banda
Sea
Aru
Islands
Flores
Sea
Surabaya
Arafura
Sea
Malang
L e s s e r   S u n d a   I s l a n d s
Bali
DILI
Denpasar
Mataram
Flores
EAST
TIMOR
Timor
Sea
Lombok
Sumbawa
Sumba
Kupang
Timor

Indonesia

Australia

AUSTRALASIA AND OCEANIA

This massive country is mostly made up of desert, which is so hot and dry that it is not suitable for farming or for people to live there. The wildest, driest, and emptiest parts of the Australian desert are sometimes called "the outback." Most of the 21.8 million people in Australia live in towns along the coast, such as Brisbane, Melbourne, and Sydney in the east, and Perth in the southwest. The first inhabitants of this continent were the Aboriginal Australians. Today, most Australians are descended from European people who migrated there from the 18th century onward. Australia has one of the world's biggest mining industries. Copper, gold, coal, and opals are all mined there. Other important Australian industries include tourism and wine making. High-quality Australian wines are exported worldwide.

Country File

Australia

97 percent of all opals are found in Australia.

INDIAN OCEAN

KIMBERLEY PLATEAU

Broome

GREAT SANDY DESERT

Port Hedland

Dampier

HAMERSLEY RANGE

GIBSON DESERT

Lake Mackay

Tropic of Capricorn

A U

WESTERN AUSTRALIA

GREAT VICTOR DESERT

Geraldton

Kalgoorlie

NULLARB

Perth ★
Fremantle
Mandurah
Bunbury

Great

SOUTHE

Cape Leeuwin

Albany

0   200   400 kilometers
0   200   400 miles

Uluru

The magnificent rock called Uluru is the top of an enormous sandstone hill that is buried beneath the desert in Northern Territory. It is also known as Ayers Rock. This is the world's biggest single rock. Uluru rises over 1,148 feet above the surrounding land and it is almost six miles long around the base. This ancient rock is a sacred place for many Aboriginal Australians.

Kangaroo

Kangaroos are mammals called marsupials. The females carry their young in a pouch. Other marsupials in Australia are wallabies, possums, and the koala. The only egg-laying mammals – the platypus and echidna – also live in Australia. They are called "monotremes."

1
2

Melville
Island

Arafura Sea

Darwin

**ARNHEM
LAND**

N

Cape
York

Did you know?

◇ Australia is the only
country that is also a
continent on its own. It
is the smallest and also
the flattest continent
in the world.

Gulf of
Carpentaria

**CAPE
YORK
PENINSULA**

Coral Sea

Great Barrier Reef

The Great Barrier Reef is made up of over 2,800 coral
reefs and is home to more than 1,500 species of fish.
It covers an enormous area – 135,136 square miles –
and is so large that it can be seen from space.

BARKLY TABLELAND

ANAMI
ESERT

**NORTHERN
TERRITORY**

Cairns

GREAT BARRIER REEF

Townsville

Australia

QUEENSLAND

*MACDONNELL
RANGES*

Alice Springs

TRALIA

Mackay

Rockhampton

Gladstone

Uluru
(Ayers Rock)
2,844 ft

*SIMPSON
DESERT*

Hervey Bay

Maroochydore-
Mooloolaba
Sunshine Coast

Koala

The koala is a marsupial
mammal that lives in
eucalyptus trees and eats
the leaves. Many of these
trees are being cut down to
make more space for roads
and buildings. Koalas are
now endangered animals.

**SOUTH
AUSTRALIA**

*Lake Eyre
North*

Coober Pedy

Toowoomba

Brisbane
Gold Coast

*Lake
Torrens*

*Lake
Frome*

IN

*Lake
Gairdner*

*FLINDERS
RANGES*

Darling River

Coffs Harbour

Port Macquarie

ian Bight

**NEW SOUTH
WALES**

GREAT DIVIDING RANGE

Broken
Hill

Newcastle

EAN

Mildura

Bathurst

Adelaide

Murray River

Wagga Wagga

Sydney

Wollongong

Nowra

Albury

CANBERRA

*Mount Kosciuszko
7,310 ft*

**AUSTRALIAN
CAPITAL
TERRITORY**

Bendigo

VICTORIA

*AUSTRALIAN
ALPS*

PACIFIC OCEAN

*Kangaroo
Island*

Ballarat

Geelong

Melbourne

Did you know?

◇ About 140 species of land snake
and 32 species of sea snake are
found in Australia.

◇ The inland taipan has the
strongest venom of any
land snake. The
venom in one
bite could kill
100 people.

*Bass
Strait*

Launceston

TASMANIA

Hobart

Sydney Opera House

Sydney is the biggest and oldest city in
Australia, and the Sydney Opera House is one
of the most famous buildings in the world.
Over 100 million people have visited it.

Pacific Islands
AUSTRALASIA AND OCEANIA

There are thousands of islands in the Pacific Ocean, and people from many cultures live there, speaking many languages. The islands are traditionally divided into these groups: Melanesia, Micronesia, and Polynesia. The earliest people in this region settled on the island of New Guinea over 40,000 years ago. In the 19th century, the islands were colonized by Europeans, who brought their own cultures, languages, and religions. Most of the islands are now part of independent countries. They rely on agriculture and fishing for their income, and some tourism. The islands also export copra, which comes from coconuts. It is made into coconut oil, which is used in soap and cosmetics.

Country File

- Fiji
- Kiribati
- Marshall Islands
- Micronesia
- Nauru
- Palau
- Papua New Guinea
- Samoa
- Solomon Islands
- Tonga
- Tuvalu
- Vanuatu

Onions, limes, ginger, garlic, and lemon juice are all traditional ingredients of many south Pacific island dishes.

Did you know?
◇ Nauru is the world's smallest republic and it has an area of 8 square miles.

◇ Throughout the Pacific islands, pit-roasted foods, including pigs, are eaten on special occasions and for religious celebrations.

Tropic of Cancer

NORTHERN MARIANA ISLANDS (to U.S.)

Marshall Isla

GUAM (to U.S.)
HAGATNA ★

Micronesia

MICRONESIA

Yap
Babeldaob
Chuuk Islands
PALIKIR
Pohnpei ★

Palau

NGERULMUD (MELEKEOK) ★

Caroline Island

PALAU

Papua New Guinea

Equator

INDONESIA

PAPUA NEW GUINEA

▲ Mount Wilhelm 14,793 ft
New Britain

PORT MORESBY ★

SC I

Guadalcanal
HONIARA

Coral Sea

Solomon Islands

AUSTRALIA

CALEDO (to F

Tropic of Capri

Vanuatu

Doria's tree kangaroo

Nine of the 11 species of tree kangaroo live in the rain forest on the island of New Guinea. The other two live in Australia. Doria's tree kangaroo is the largest one, weighing nearly 282 pounds. Like all kangaroos, it is a marsupial.

Did you know?
◇ The Pacific Ocean has lots of volcanic activity. Most of the Pacific islands were formed by volcanoes under the sea.

Fishing

The people of the Pacific islands fish mainly to feed themselves, but many fish are also caught in the northern Pacific by big fishing boats from Japan, South Korea, Taiwan, and the U.S.A. Tuna is a prized fish and the finest tuna can sell for thousands of dollars per fish, especially in Japan. Today much of the commercial fishing of tuna is done using long fishing lines instead of nets.

Papua New Guinea

New Guinea is the second largest island in the world, and Papua New Guinea takes up the eastern half, as well as several smaller islands. About 80 percent of the population live in groups in the countryside. People live as they have done for many hundreds of years, with traditional ways of life, customs, and beliefs.

Did you know?
◇ Papua New Guinea has more ethnic variety than any other country, and it has more than 820 living languages.

◇ Sugarcane probably first came from New Guinea, the island partly occupied by Papua New Guinea.

◇ The coconut tree is called "the tree of life" by many islanders because every part of it is used or eaten.

Cyclones

The Pacific islands suffer from cyclones every year. These strong winds blow at over 74 miles an hour and can cause serious damage. In other parts of the world they are called typhoons or hurricanes. Palm trees can bend in the wind and survive cyclones.

The International Dateline is an imaginary line that separates two calendar days. This means that the date to the east of the line is always one day ahead of the date to the west of the line.

Farming

Many Pacific islands are mountainous but people are able to grow some food crops along the coast. Coconuts, sweet potatoes, and bananas all grow well in the hot, humid climate of the Pacific. Cocoa and coffee are both important crops in Papua New Guinea.

Green turtle

These endangered turtles live in warm waters all around the Pacific. They are some of the biggest turtles and can reach almost five feet in length. The adults feed on sea grasses and algae, but the young eat jellyfish, shellfish, and sponges.

Did you know?

◈ In Papua New Guinea and other islands in Melanesia, a language called Tok Pisin has developed, based on English. Communities in this area use it when they talk to each other because they do not understand each other's own, native language.

MIDWAY ISLANDS (to U.S.)

Hawaiian Islands (to U.S.)

Kauai
Oahu   Maui
Hawaii

WAKE ISLAND (to U.S.)

Nauru

Tuvalu

JOHNSTON ATOLL (to U.S.)

N

Samoa

MARSHALL ISLANDS

Ratak Chain

Ralik Chain

MAJURO

PACIFIC OCEAN

KINGMAN REEF (to U.S.)

PALMYRA ATOLL (to U.S.)

Line Islands

Kiritimati

Equator

NAURU   Tarawa
BAIRIKI

Tungaru

BAKER & HOWLAND ISLANDS (to U.S.)

JARVIS ISLAND (to U.S.)

KIRIBATI

Phoenix Islands

KIRIBATI

Millennium Island

Marquesas Islands

Micronesia

TUVALU

Polynesia

Santa Cruz Islands

Funafuti
FUNAFUTI

TOKELAU (to New Zealand)

Northern Cook Islands

VANUATU

WALLIS AND FUTUNA (to France)   Wallis
MATA'UTU   Futuna

SAMOA
APIA

PAGO PAGO
AMERICAN SAMOA (to U.S.)

COOK ISLANDS (to New Zealand)

Bora-Bora

Tuamotu Islands

Vanua Levu

Melanesia

Efate
PORT-VILA

Viti Levu   SUVA

TONGA

NIUE (to New Zealand)
★ ALOFI

Society Islands

Tahiti   PAPEETE

FRENCH POLYNESIA (to France)

Lau Group

Loyalty Islands

New Caledonia

NOUMÉA

FIJI

NUKU'ALOFA
Tongatapu

Southern Cook Islands

Rarotonga
AVARUA

Austral Islands

Gambier Islands

PITCAIRN ISLANDS (to U.K.)

NORFOLK ISLAND (to Australia)

Fiji

Tonga   Kiribati

0   250   500 kilometers

0   250   500 miles

Tasman Sea

NEW ZEALAND

North Island

WELLINGTON

South Island

Polynesia

The beautiful island of Bora-Bora is in French Polynesia, an overseas territory of France. Bora-Bora is one of the main tourist destinations of French Polynesia. Its highest peak is Mount Otemanu, which is 2,385 feet high.

New Zealand

AUSTRALASIA AND OCEANIA

Country File

New Zealand

This country in the south Pacific Ocean is similar in size to the United Kingdom. It consists of two main islands – North Island and South Island – and several smaller islands. New Zealand is well known for its amazing scenery. The landscape includes mountains, volcanoes, long sandy beaches, deep fjords, and lush rain forests. It has cool, wet winters and warm, wet summers. New Zealand is one of the world's least populated countries, with almost 4.3 million people. The first people to settle there around 1,000 years ago were the Polynesians. They became known as the Maoris. For the past 160 years people have migrated there from many countries. Tourism, fishing, and hi-tech manufacturing are important industries.

Auckland

The largest city in New Zealand is Auckland, and about one-third of the population lives there. More than 60 percent of residents are descended from Europeans and 14 percent are Maori. This city is very popular with immigrants. Nobody in Auckland lives more than half an hour away from a beach, and the weather is warm all year round.

Did you know?

◇ New Zealand was one of the last places on Earth to be inhabited by people.

◇ Almost one-third of New Zealand is covered by forest. Many of the forests contain unusual species of trees that are found only on these islands, such as kauri trees, which are some of the oldest trees on Earth.

◇ Wine making is a fast-growing industry in New Zealand, and the wines are exported worldwide.

This wooden Maori Tiki carving represents the first man. Tiki carvings are thought of as powerful good luck symbols.

Whale watching

One of the best places to see whales and dolphins in the wild is near the town of Kaikoura, on the east coast of South Island. New Zealand's whales, dolphins, and seals are protected, and visitors from all over the world travel to Kaikoura to see them. The whale is a spiritual symbol for the Maoris.

Aoraki/Mount Cook

The highest mountain in New Zealand is Aoraki/Mount Cook in the Southern Alps. It is 12,316 feet high. In Maori legend, these mountains are Aoraki and his three brothers, who are the sons of the Sky Father. They were stranded in their canoe and were frozen by the cold south wind. Their canoe became South Island.

Tasman Sea

Westport

Greymouth

South Island

Aoraki/ Mount Cook 12,316 ft ▲

SOUTHERN ALPS

Haast

Ashburton

Milford Sound

Wanaka

Timaru

Lake Wakatipu

Queenstown

Waitaki

Canterb. Ri.

Lake Te Anau

Oamaru

FIORDLAND

Te Anau

Mataura

Clutha

Dunedir

Invercargill

Foveaux Strait

Stewart Island

North Cape

Apples and pears have been grown in the region around Nelson since the 1850s. Most of the fruit is exported to Europe.

Did you know?

◇ The New Zealand rugby union team is known as the "All Blacks." All the players perform the *haka*, a traditional Maori dance, before every game.

◇ Aoraki/Mount Cook used to be about 33 feet taller than it is now. In 1991, a huge amount of rock and ice fell off the summit in a landslide.

Kiwi

The kiwi is the national symbol of New Zealand. This bird is around the size of a chicken. It cannot fly, so it is at risk from predators, especially domestic cats and dogs. There are only around 70,000 of these birds left in the wild.

Whangarei

Great Barrier Island

0   100   200 kilometers

0   100   200 miles

Auckland

Manurewa

Bay of Plenty

Hamilton

Tauranga

East Cape

Lake Rotorua

Whakatane

Rotorua

Lake Taupo

Taupo

Gisborne

North Island

New Plymouth

Cape Egmont

Mount Ruapehu 9,177 ft

Mount Taranaki 8,261 ft

Napier

Wanganui

Hastings

Rangitikei

Geysers and springs

The area around Rotorua on North Island is famous for its geysers, hot springs, and boiling mud, which are all heated deep inside the Earth. Geysers have a spiritual meaning for the Maoris and almost all have names. The largest is Pohutu, which shoots up to 98 feet into the air.

NEW

pe well

ZEALAND

Cook Strait

Masterton

Lower Hutt

★ WELLINGTON

Cape Palliser

enheim

Wairau

Clarence

Kairkoura

N

PACIFIC OCEAN

New Zealand

Waimakariri

ristchurch

Banks Peninsula

Did you know?

◇ About two-thirds of New Zealand's energy comes from hydroelectricity, which is produced by its fast-flowing rivers. The water is used to turn huge wheels called turbines, which in turn power an electric generator.

◇ New Zealand produces about 25% of the world's "strong wool," which is used to make wool products that need to be hard-wearing, such as carpets and rugs.

Milford Sound

One of the most beautiful places in New Zealand is Milford Sound in the fjord lands of South Island. It is over nine miles long and is surrounded by sheer cliffs rising more than 3,937 feet on each side. There are lush rain forests clinging to the sides of the fjord, and seals, dolphins, and penguins swim in the waters. One of the world's most popular walks, the Milford Track, finishes here.

There are about 31.9 million sheep in New Zealand. New Zealand lamb is famous all over the world.

Hooker's sea lion

These sea lions are found only in New Zealand, mostly around the Auckland Islands. In the breeding season, a male lives with a group of up to 25 females. These sea lions can swim over 77 miles to find food, which includes squid, crabs, crayfish, and fish.

USA
(Alaska)

Chukchi
Sea

Wrangel
Island

Bering Strait

Arctic Circle

Limit of summer pack ice

Limit of permanent ice cap

East
Siberian
Sea

New
Siberian
Islands

RUSSIAN FEDERATION

Beaufort
Sea

Banks
Island

Victoria
Island

Melville
Island

Queen
Elizabeth
Islands

Ellesmere
Island

ARCTIC
OCEAN

North Pole •

Laptev
Sea

Taymyr Peninsula

Severnaya
Zemlya

Kara
Sea

Qaanaaq

Knud
Rasmussen
Land

Baffin
Bay

Wandel
Sea

Franz
Josef
Land

Novaya Zemlya

Limit of permanent ice cap

SVALBARD
(to Norway)

Limit of summer pack ice

Limit of winter pack ice

Barents
Sea

Aasiat
Sisimiut
Maniitsoq
NUUK ★

Ilulissat

GREENLAND
(to Denmark)

Kong Christian IX Land

Gunnbjørn
Fjeld
12,139 ft

Ittoqqortoormiit

Greenland
Sea

North Cape

Kola
Peninsula

NORWAY

Qaqortoq

Tasiilaq

Nunap Isua

Denmark Strait

Norwegian
Sea

FINLAND

Arctic Circle

REYKJAVIK ★ ICELAND

CANADA

Baffin Island

Davis Strait

| 0 | 400 | 800 kilometers |
| 0 | 400 | 800 miles |

The Arctic

ASIA, EUROPE, AND NORTH AMERICA

The Arctic is a huge area with the North Pole at its center. It is not a continent or a country but includes the Arctic Ocean and the most northern parts of Asia, North America, and Europe. During winter, much of the Arctic Ocean is covered by pack ice around 13 feet thick. During the short summers the ice melts and the area of pack ice shrinks. It grows again when winter returns and temperatures drop to -76°F. Even though the climate is cold, people have lived in the Arctic for thousands of years. The Sami and Inuit people were originally nomads who survived by herding animals and hunting. Today most people live in new towns, but some still live a traditional life.

Polar bear

There are 21–25,000 polar bears in the Arctic. These animals are now a threatened species. As the Arctic pack ice continues to melt, polar bears are finding it difficult to hunt for food because they have to swim so far between the bits of ice. Many polar bears are dying as they search for food.

Did you know?

◇ The Arctic Ocean is the smallest ocean in the world. It measures about 5.4 million square miles.

◇ By 2030 the Arctic may have ice-free summers because so much ice is melting in summer and not refreezing in winter.

Inuit people once lived by fishing, herding, and hunting whales, bears, and seals. Many still wear clothes made of fur to keep them warm.

Northern lights

The *aurora borealis*, or the northern lights, are caused by solar winds reacting with the Earth's upper atmosphere. This colorful effect in the sky can also be seen around the South Pole, where it is known as the southern lights, or *aurora australis*.

Antarctica
ANTARCTICA

This is the fifth largest continent and it is almost twice the size of the U.S.A. Antarctica has a harsh, cold climate and it is the windiest place on Earth. Almost all of Antarctica is covered with a sheet of ice. On average, the ice is almost one mile thick, and it is thousands of years old. The ice contains most of the fresh water on Earth. Under the ice, the land contains oil and other minerals, including gold, iron ore, and coal. Huge blocks of ice often break off the edge of the sheet and float away as icebergs. To protect this wilderness and its wildlife, 46 nations have signed an agreement called the Antarctic Treaty. They agree not to carry out any mining or put a military station there. Antarctica is the only continent where people do not live all year round.

Did you know?
◈ In winter the temperatures in Antarctica can drop to below -112°F.

◈ Antarctica is unusual because it is not owned by any country.

Cold science
Groups of scientists, tourists, and explorers are allowed to visit Antarctica. Many things are studied in Antarctica, including how plants and animals can survive there.

Humpbacks and other whales visit the icy seas of Antarctica. When a whale leaps out of the water it is known as "breaching."

Emperor penguin
The only penguins that breed in Antarctica during the bitter cold winter are emperor penguins. They weigh over 66 pounds and are the tallest penguins, at almost four feet high. They walk over 74 miles to their breeding grounds.

Did you know?
◈ The weight of the ice in Antarctica has pushed the land below sea level.

0 500 kilometers
0 500 miles

AALBORG—BENIN

Index to the maps

In this atlas there is an **Index to the maps** *on page 60 and a* **General index** *on page 68.*

Place name index

The **Index to the maps** *lists all the names that appear on the maps. Each name is followed by a description, its location, a page number, and a grid reference number. Town names do not have a description.*

place name   description   location

Anatolia *physical region* Turkey **10 D5**

page number

grid reference

To find our example "Anatolia," first go to the page shown – p.10, then find the letter "D" and number "5" around the border of the page. Trace a line down from 'D' and a line across from "5." The lines meet at the precise square on the grid in which "Anatolia" can be found.

• • A • •

Aalborg Denmark **33 L10**
Aasiat Greenland **58 B6**
Aberdeen Scotland, U.K. **35 O2**
Abha Saudi Arabia **43 N10**
Abidjan Ivory Coast **28 H10**
Abu Dhabi *capital city* United Arab Emirates **43 Q8**
Abuja *capital city* Nigeria **28 J10**
Acapulco Mexico **24 G8**
Accra *capital city* Ghana **28 H10**
Aconcagua, Cerro *mountain* Argentina **27 O9**
A Coruña Spain **35 M8**
Adana Turkey **43 L3**
Ad Dahna *desert* Saudi Arabia **43 O7**
Ad Damman Saudi Arabia **43 P7**
Addis Ababa *capital city* Ethiopia **29 O9**
Adelaide *state capital* South Australia **53 M9**
Aden Yemen **43 N12**
Aden, Gulf of *sea feature* NW Indian Ocean **10 E7**
Adriatic Sea *sea* Mediterranean Sea **37 O8**
Aegean Sea *sea* Mediterranean Sea **39 O10**
Afghanistan *country* C Asia **45 M10**
Africa *continent* **10 C7**
Agadez Niger **28 J8**
Agra India **47 N4**
Ahaggar *plateau* Algeria **28 I7**
Ahmadabad India **47 M6**
Ahvaz Iran **43 O5**
Ajaccio France **35 R9**
Aksai Chin *disputed territory* S Asia **47 O1**
Aktau Kazakhstan **44 I6**
Aktobe Kazakhstan **45 K4**
Akureyri Iceland **33 L1**
Alabama *state* U.S.A. **23 P8**
Alai Range *mountain range* Kyrgyzstan/Tajikistan **45 O8**
Alakol, Lake *lake* Kazakhstan **45 R5**
Aland Islands *island group* Finland **33 O8**
Alaska *state* U.S.A. **22 G9**
Alaska, Gulf of *sea feature* N Pacific Ocean **22 G10**
Alaska Range *mountain range* U.S.A. **11 M3**
Albacete Spain **35 O11**
Albania *country* SE Europe **39 M9**
Albany Western Australia **52 G10**
Albany *state capital* New York, U.S.A. **23 R5**
Alberta *province* Canada **20 H7**
Albuquerque New Mexico, U.S.A. **23 K8**
Albury New South Wales, Australia **53 O10**
Aldan *river* Russia **41 O8**
Aleppo Syria **43 L4**
Aleutian Islands *island group* U.S.A. **11 L4**
Alexander Island *island* Antarctica **59 N8**
Alexandria Egypt **29 M5**
Algeria *country* N Africa **28 I6**
Algiers *capital city* Algeria **28 I4**
Al Hufuf Saudi Arabia **43 P7**
Alicante Spain **35 O11**
Alice Springs Northern Territory, Australia **53 L6**
Al Kut Iraq **43 O5**
Allahabad India **47 O5**
Almaty Kazakhstan **45 Q6**
Al Mukalla Yemen **43 P11**
Alofi *capital city* Niue **55 N8**
Alps *mountain range* C Europe **10 C4**
Altai Mountains *mountain range* C Asia **10 G4**
Altamira Brazil **27 Q4**
Altun Shan *mountain range* China **48 H6**
Amazon *river* C South America **27 Q4**
Amazon Basin *basin* C South America **27 O4**
Ambon Indonesia **51 O10**
American Samoa *U.S. territory* C Pacific Ocean **55 N7**
Amiens France **35 P5**
Amman *capital city* Jordan **43 L5**
Amritsar India **47 M3**
Amsterdam *capital city* Netherlands **35 Q4**
Amu Darya *river* C Asia **45 M9**
Amundsen Sea *sea* Southern Ocean **59 N10**
Amur *river* China/Russia **10 I4**
Anápolis Brazil **27 Q6**
Anatolia *physical region* Turkey **10 D5**
Anchorage Alaska, U.S.A. **22 G10**
Andaman Islands *island group* India **47 S9**
Andaman Sea *sea* NE Indian Ocean **50 F7**
Andes *mountain range* W South America **27 M5**
Andijon Uzbekistan **45 P8**
Andorra *country* SW Europe **35 O9**
Andros Island *island* Bahamas **25 M6**
Angara *river* Russia **41 K9**
Angel Falls *waterfall* Venezuela **27 P3**
Angkor Wat *archaeological site* Cambodia **50 I5**
Angola *country* S Africa **30 I7**
Anguilla *U.K. territory* Caribbean **25 R7**
Ankara *capital city* Turkey **43 K2**
An Nafud *desert* Saudi Arabia **43 M6**
An Najaf Iraq **43 N5**
Annamese Cordillera *mountain range* SE Asia **50 I4**
Annapolis *state capital* Maryland, U.S.A. **23 R6**
An Nasiriyah Iraq **43 O6**
Anshan China **49 O5**
Antalya Turkey **43 K3**
Antananarivo *capital city* Madagascar **31 O8**
Antarctica *continent* **59 P8**
Antarctic Peninsula *peninsula* Antarctica **59 N8**
Anticosti Island *island* Canada **21 Q8**
Antigua & Barbuda *country* Caribbean **25 R7**
Antofagasta Chile **27 N7**
Antwerp Belgium **35 Q5**
Aoraki *mountain* New Zealand **56 I9**
Apennines *mountain range* Italy **37 M7**
Apia *capital city* Samoa **55 N8**
Appalachian Mountains *mountain range* U.S.A. **23 P7**
Arabian Peninsula *peninsula* SW Asia **43 M7**
Arabian Sea *sea* NW Indian Ocean **10 F6**
Aracaju Brazil **27 S5**
Arafura Sea *sea* SW Pacific Ocean **10 I8**
Araguaia *river* Brazil **27 Q5**
Arak Iran **43 P4**
Aral Sea *lake* Kazakhstan/Uzbekistan **45 L6**
Ararat, Mt *mountain* Turkey **43 N2**
Aras *river* SW Asia **43 O3**
Archangel Russia **40 G6**
Arctic Ocean *ocean* **58 C3**
Arequipa Peru **27 N6**
Argentina *country* S South America **27 O9**
Arhus Denmark **33 L10**
Arica Chile **27 N6**
Arizona *state* U.S.A. **22 I8**
Arkansas *state* U.S.A. **23 N7**
Arkansas *river* U.S.A. **23 N8**
Armenia *country* SW Asia **43 N2**
Arnhem Land *physical region* Australia **53 L2**
Ar Rub' Al Khali *desert* Saudi Arabia **43 O9**
Arta Greece **39 N10**
Aruba *Dutch territory* Caribbean **25 P9**
Aru Islands *island group* Indonesia **51 Q11**
Ascension Island *U.K. territory* C Atlantic Ocean **12 A8**
Ascension Island *island* C Atlantic Ocean **10 B8**
Asgabat *capital city* Turkmenistan **45 K9**
Ashburton New Zealand **56 J9**
Asia *continent* **10 H4**
Asmara *capital city* Eritrea **29 O8**
As Sib Oman **43 R8**
Astana *capital city* Kazakhstan **45 O3**
Astrakhan' Russia **40 E9**
Asunción *capital city* Paraguay **27 P7**
Aswan Egypt **29 N7**
Atacama Desert *desert* Chile **27 O7**
Athabasca *river* Canada **20 H8**
Athabasca, Lake *lake* Canada **20 I7**
Athens *capital city* Greece **39 O10**
Atlanta *state capital* Georgia, U.S.A. **23 P8**
Atlantic Ocean *ocean* **10 B9**
Atlas Mountains *mountain range* NW Africa **28 H5**
At Taif Saudi Arabia **43 M9**
Atyrau Kazakhstan **44 J5**
Auckland New Zealand **57 L3**
Augusta *state capital* Maine, U.S.A. **23 S4**
Aurangabad India **47 M7**
Austin *state capital* Texas, U.S.A. **23 M9**
Austral Islands *island group* French Polynesia **55 P9**
Australia *country* **52 J6**
Australia *continent* **10 I9**
Australian Alps *mountain range* Australia **53 O10**
Australian Capital Territory *territory* Australia **53 P10**
Austria *country* C Europe **37 O5**
Avarua *capital city* Cook Islands **55 O9**
Ayers Rock *see* Uluru
Azerbaijan *country* SW Asia **43 O2**
Azores *island group* Portugal **34 I11**
Azov, Sea of *sea* Black Sea **39 S6**

• • B • •

Babeldaob *island* Palau **54 H5**
Bab el Mandeb *sea feature* NW Indian Ocean **43 N12**
Babruysk Belarus **39 P2**
Bacau Romania **39 P6**
Bacolod Philippines **51 N6**
Baffin Bay *sea feature* NW Atlantic Ocean **58 B5**
Baffin Island *island* Canada **21 M4**
Baghdad *capital city* Iraq **43 N5**
Baghlan Afghanistan **45 O10**
Baguio Philippines **51 M4**
Bahamas *country* Caribbean **25 N6**
Bahamas *island group* Caribbean **11 Q6**
Bahía Blanca Argentina **27 P10**
Bahrain *country* SW Asia **43 P7**
Baikal, Lake *lake* Russia **41 L10**
Bairiki *capital city* Kiribati **55 L6**
Baja California *peninsula* Mexico **24 D3**
Baker & Howland Islands *U.S. territory* C Pacific Ocean **55 M6**
Baku *capital city* Azerbaijan **43 P2**
Balearic Islands *island group* Spain **35 P11**
Bali *island* Indonesia **51 L11**
Balikpapan Indonesia **51 L9**
Balkanabat Turkmenistan **44 J8**
Balkan Mountains *mountain range* Bulgaria **39 O8**
Balkh Afghanistan **45 N9**
Balkhash, Lake *lake* Kazakhstan **45 P5**
Ballarat Victoria, Australia **53 N10**
Balsas *river* Mexico **24 G7**
Baltic Sea *sea* NE Atlantic Ocean **33 O11**
Baltimore Maryland, U.S.A. **23 R6**
Bamako *capital city* Mali **28 G9**
Bamian Afghanistan **45 N10**
Banda Aceh Indonesia **50 F7**
Bandar Seri Begawan *capital city* Brunei **51 L8**
Bandar-e' Abbas Iran **43 R7**
Bandar-e Bushehr Iran **43 P6**
Bandarlampung Indonesia **50 I10**
Banda Sea *sea* W Pacific Ocean **51 O10**
Bandung Indonesia **50 J11**
Bangalore India **47 N9**
Bangka *island* Indonesia **50 I9**
Bangkok *capital city* Thailand **50 H5**
Bangladesh *country* S Asia **47 R5**
Bangui *capital city* Central African Republic **29 L10**
Banja Luka Bosnia & Herzegovina **39 L7**
Banjarmasin Indonesia **51 L10**
Banjul *capital city* Gambia **28 F9**
Banks Island *island* Canada **20 I3**
Banks Peninsula *peninsula* New Zealand **57 K9**
Banska Bystrica Slovakia **37 Q5**
Baotou China **49 M6**
Barbados *country* Caribbean **25 S8**
Barcelona Spain **35 P9**
Barcelona Venezuela **27 O2**
Barents Sea *sea* Arctic Ocean **58 E6**
Bari Italy **37 P9**
Barinas Venezuela **27 N2**
Barisan Mountains *mountain range* Indonesia **50 G8**
Barkley Tableland *plateau* Australia **53 L3**
Barnaul Russia **40 J10**
Barquisimeto Venezuela **27 N2**
Barranquilla Colombia **27 N2**
Basel Switzerland **37 L5**
Basra Iraq **43 O6**
Bassein Burma **50 F4**
Bass Strait *sea feature* Australia **53 O11**
Batdambang Cambodia **50 I5**
Bathurst New South Wales, Australia **53 P9**
Baton Rouge *state capital* Louisiana, U.S.A. **23 O9**
Beaufort Sea *sea* Arctic Ocean **58 B2**
Beijing *capital city* China **49 N6**
Beira Mozambique **31 M9**
Beirut *capital city* Lebanon **43 L4**
Belarus *country* E Europe **39 P2**
Belém Brazil **27 R4**
Belfast *province capital* Northern Ireland, U.K. **35 N3**
Belgium *country* NW Europe **35 Q5**
Belgrade *capital city* Serbia **39 M7**
Belize *country* Central America **25 K8**
Belize City Belize **25 K8**
Bellingshausen Sea *sea* Southern Ocean **59 N9**
Belmopan *capital city* Belize **25 K8**
Belo Horizonte Brazil **27 R7**
Bendigo Victoria, Australia **53 N10**
Bengal, Bay of *sea feature* NE Indian Ocean **10 G6**
Benghazi Libya **29 L5**
Bengkulu Indonesia **50 H10**
Benin *country* W Africa **28 I9**

Bergen   Norway 33 K8
Bering Sea   *sea* N Pacific Ocean 11 L4
Bering Strait   *sea feature* Arctic
    Ocean/Pacific Ocean 58 C1
Berkner Island   *island* Antarctica 59 O8
Berlin   *capital city* Germany 37 N2
Bermuda   *U.K. territory* W Atlantic Ocean
    13 R5
Bermuda   *island* W Atlantic Ocean 11 R5
Bern   *capital city* Switzerland 37 L6
Bhopal   India 47 N6
Bhubaneshwar   India 47 Q7
Bhutan   *country* S Asia 47 R4
Bialystok   Poland 37 R2
Bien Hoa   Vietnam 50 J6
Bié Plateau   *plateau* Angola 30 J7
Bilbao   Spain 35 N8
Biratnagar   Nepal 47 Q4
Birmingham   England, U.K. 35 O4
Birmingham   Alabama, U.S.A. 23 P8
Biscay, Bay of   *sea feature* NE Atlantic Ocean
    35 N7
Bishkek   *capital city* Kyrgyzstan 45 P7
Bismarck   *state capital* North Dakota, U.S.A.
    23 L4
Bissau   *capital city* Guinea-Bissau 28 F9
Bitola   Macedonia 39 N9
Black Forest   *physical region* Germany 37 L5
Black Sea   *sea* Asia/Europe 10 D5
Black Sea Lowland   *lowland* SE Europe
    39 Q6
Blanc, Mont   *mountain* France/Italy 35 R7
Blantyre   Malawi 31 M8
Blenheim   New Zealand 57 L7
Bloemfontein   *capital city* South Africa
    31 K10
Blue Nile   *river* Ethiopia/Sudan 29 N9
Bodo   Norway 33 N4
Bogor   Indonesia 50 I11
Bogotá   *capital city* Colombia 27 N3
Boise   *state capital* Idaho, U.S.A. 22 I4
Bolivia   *country* C South America 27 O6
Bologna   Italy 37 N7
Bonn   Germany 37 L3
Bora Bora   *island* French Polynesia 55 P8
Bordeaux   France 35 O8
Borneo   *island* SE Asia 51 K9
Bornholm   *island* Denmark 33 N11
Bosnia & Herzegovina   *country* SE Europe
    39 L7
Boston   Massachusetts, U.S.A. 23 S4
Bothnia, Gulf of   *sea feature* NE Atlantic
    Ocean 33 O7
Botswana   *country* S Africa 31 K9
Braga   Portugal 35 L9
Brahmaputra   *river* S Asia 10 G6
Braila   Romania 39 P7
Branco   *river* Brazil 27 P3
Brasília   *capital city* Brazil 27 R6
Brasov   Romania 39 O6
Bratislava   *capital city* Slovakia 37 P5
Brazil   *country* South America 27 O5
Brazilian Highlands   *mountain range*
    Brazil 27 R6
Brazzaville   *capital city* Congo 30 I5
Bremen   Germany 37 M2
Brest   Belarus 39 O3
Brest   France 35 N6
Brisbane   *state capital* Queensland,
    Australia 53 Q7
Bristol   England, U.K. 35 O5
Britain   *island* U.K. 10 B4
British Columbia   *province* Canada 20 G7
British Indian Ocean Territory   *U.K. territory*
    C Indian Ocean 12 F8
British Virgin Islands   *U.K. territory*
    Caribbean 25 R6
Brno   Czech Republic 37 P4
Broken Hill   New South Wales,
    Australia 53 N8
Broome   Western Australia 52 H4
Brunei   *country* SE Asia 51 K8
Brussels   *capital city* Belgium 35 Q5
Bucaramanga   Colombia 27 N2
Bucharest   *capital city* Romania 39 P7
Budapest   *capital city* Hungary 39 M5
Buenos Aires   *capital city* Argentina 27 P9
Buffalo   New York, U.S.A. 23 Q5
Bujumbura   *capital city* Burundi 31 L5

Bulawayo   Zimbabwe 31 K9
Bulgaria   *country* SE Europe 39 O8
Bunbury   Western Australia 52 G9
Buraydah   Saudi Arabia 43 N7
Burgas   Bulgaria 39 P8
Burkina Faso   *country* W Africa 28 H9
Burma   *country* SE Asia 50 G3
Bursa   Turkey 42 J2
Buru   *island* Indonesia 51 O10
Burundi   *country* C Africa 31 L5
Buxoro   Uzbekistan 45 M8
Bydgoszcz   Poland 37 P2

•• C ••

Cabinda   *province* Angola 12 C8
Cagayan de Oro   Philippines 51 N7
Cagliari   Italy 37 L10
Cairns   Queensland, Australia 53 O4
Cairo   *capital city* Egypt 29 N5
Calgary   Alberta, Canada 20 H9
Cali   Colombia 27 M3
California   *state* U.S.A. 22 G5
California, Gulf of   *sea feature* E Pacific
    Ocean 24 D4
Callao   Peru 27 M5
Camaguey   Cuba 25 N6
Cambodia   *country* SE Asia 50 I5
Cameroon   *country* W Africa 29 K11
Campeche   Mexico 24 J7
Campeche, Bay of   *sea feature* Mexico
    24 I7
Campinas   Brazil 27 R7
Campo Grande   Brazil 27 Q7
Canada   *country* N North America 20 J7
Canadian Shield   *physical region* Canada
    20 J6
Canary Islands   *island group* Spain
    34 I12
Canberra   *capital city* Australia 53 P10
Cancun   Mexico 25 K7
Canterbury Bight   *sea feature* New Zealand
    56 J10
Can Tho   Vietnam 50 I6
Cape Town   *capital city* South Africa 30 J11
Cape Verde   *country* W Africa 28 D8
Cape Verde Islands   *island group* W Africa
    10 A7
Cape York Peninsula   *peninsula* Australia
    53 N3
Caracas   *capital city* Venezuela 27 O2
Carajás   Brazil 27 Q4
Cardiff   *capital city* Wales, U.K. 35 N5
Caribbean Sea   *sea* W Atlantic Ocean
    25 N9
Carney Island   *island* Antarctica 59 N10
Caroline Islands   *island group* Micronesia
    54 I5
Carpathian Mountains   *mountain range*
    E Europe 10 D4
Carpentaria, Gulf of   *sea feature* W Pacific
    Ocean 53 M3
Carson City   *state capital* Nevada, U.S.A.
    22 H5
Cartagena   Colombia 27 M2
Casablanca   Morocco 28 G5
Caspian Depression   *lowland*
    Kazakhstan/Russia 44 J4
Caspian Sea   *lake* Asia/Europe 10 E5
Catania   Italy 37 O11
Catanzaro   Italy 37 P11
Caucasus   *mountain range* Asia/Europe
    10 E5
Cayenne   *capital city* French Guiana 27 Q3
Cayman Islands   *U.K. territory* Caribbean
    25 L7
Cebu   Philippines 51 N6
Celebes Sea   *sea* W Pacific Ocean 51 M8
Central African Republic   *country* C Africa
    29 L10
Central Makran Range   *mountain range*
    Pakistan 46 J4
Central Range   *mountain range*
    Indonesia/Papua New Guinea 51 R10
Central Russian Upland   *plateau*
    Russia 40 F7
Central Siberian Plateau   *plateau*
    Russia 41 K7
Ceram   *island* Indonesia 51 O10
Chad   *country* C Africa 29 L8
Chad, Lake   *lake* C Africa 29 K9

Chagos Archipelago   *island group* C Indian
    Ocean 10 F8
Chambal   *river* India 47 N5
Changchun   China 49 P4
Changsha   China 49 M9
Channel Islands   *U.K. territory* NW Europe
    35 N6
Charleston   *state capital* West Virginia, U.S.A.
    23 Q6
Charlotte   North Carolina, U.S.A. 23 Q7
Charlottetown   *province capital* Prince
    Edward Island, Canada 21 Q9
Chatham Islands   *island group* New Zealand
    11 L10
Chelyabinsk   Russia 40 H8
Chenab   *river* India/Pakistan 47 M2
Chengdu   China 49 K9
Chennai   India 47 O9
Cherkasy   Ukraine 39 Q4
Chernihiv   Ukraine 39 Q3
Chernivtsi   Ukraine 39 O5
Chernobyl'   Ukraine 39 Q3
Cherskogo, Khrebet   *mountain range* Russia
    41 O6
Cheyenne   *state capital* Wyoming, U.S.A.
    23 K6
Chiang Mai   Thailand 50 H4
Chicago   Illinois, U.S.A. 23 O5
Chiclayo   Peru 27 M5
Chicoutimi   Québec, Canada 21 O9
Chihuahua   Mexico 24 F4
Chile   *country* S South America 27 N8
Chiloé, Isla de   *island* Chile 27 N10
China   *country* E Asia 48 I8
Chindwin   *river* Burma 50 G2
Chisinau   *capital city* Moldova 39 P6
Chita   Russia 41 M10
Chittagong   Bangladesh 47 S6
Chon Buri   Thailand 50 H5
Ch'ongjin   North Korea 49 Q5
Chongqing   China 49 L9
Choybalsan   Mongolia 49 M3
Christchurch   New Zealand 57 K9
Christmas Island   *Australian territory*
    NE Indian Ocean 12 H8
Chukchi Sea   *sea* Arctic Ocean 58 C2
Churchill   *river* Canada 21 K7
Chuuk Islands   *island group* Micronesia
    54 I5
Cincinnati   Ohio, U.S.A. 23 P6
Ciudad del Este   Paraguay 27 Q7
Ciudad Guayana   Venezuela 27 O2
Ciudad Juarez   Mexico 24 F3
Ciudad Victoria   Mexico 24 H6
Clarence   *river* New Zealand 57 K8
Clermont-Ferrand   France 35 Q7
Cleveland   Ohio, U.S.A. 23 Q5
Clipperton Island   *French territory* E Pacific
    Ocean 13 O7
Cluj-Napoca   Romania 39 O6
Clutha   *river* New Zealand 56 I11
Coast Mountains   *mountain range*
    Canada/U.S.A. 11 N4
Coats Land   *physical region* Antarctica
    59 P7
Cochabamba   Bolivia 27 O6
Cocos Islands   *Australian territory* NE Indian
    Ocean 12 G8
Cocos Islands   *island group* NE Indian
    Ocean 10 G8
Coffs Harbour   New South Wales, Australia
    53 Q8
Coimbatore   India 47 N10
Coimbra   Portugal 35 L10
Colima   Mexico 24 F7
Cologne   Germany 37 L3
Colombia   *country* N South America 27 N3
Colombo   *capital city* Sri Lanka 47 O11
Colon   Panama 25 M10
Colorado   *state* U.S.A. 23 K7
Colorado   *river* Mexico/U.S.A. 11 O5
Colorado Springs   Colorado, U.S.A. 23 K6
Columbia   *state capital* South Carolina,
    U.S.A. 23 Q8
Columbus   *state capital* Ohio, U.S.A. 23 Q6
Comoros   *country* SE Africa 31 N7
Comoros Islands   *island group* SE Africa
    10 E8
Conakry   *capital city* Guinea 28 F9
Concepción   Chile 27 N9

Conchos   *river* Mexico 24 F4
Concord   *state capital* New Hampshire,
    U.S.A. 23 S4
Congo   *country* C Africa 30 I5
Congo   *river* C Africa 30 I5
Congo Basin   *basin* C Africa 30 J4
Congo, Democratic Republic of   *country*
    C Africa 30 I5
Connecticut   *state* U.S.A. 23 S5
Constanta   Romania 39 P7
Constantine   Algeria 28 J4
Coober Pedy   South Australia 53 L7
Cook Islands   *N.Z. territory* C Pacific Ocean
    55 O8
Cook Islands   *island group* C Pacific Ocean
    11 M8
Cook, Mount   *see* Aoraki
Cook Strait   *sea feature* New Zealand 57 L7
Copenhagen   *capital city* Denmark 33 M11
Coral Sea   *sea* SW Pacific Ocean 10 J8
Córdoba   Argentina 27 O8
Córdoba   Spain 35 N11
Corfu   *island* Greece 39 M10
Cork   Ireland 35 M4
Coromandel Coast   *coast* India 47 P10
Corrientes   Argentina 27 P8
Corsica   *island* France 35 S9
Costa Brava   *coast* Spain 35 Q9
Costa Rica   *country* Central America 25 L10
Cozumel, Isla   *island* Mexico 25 K7
Craiova   Romania 39 O7
Crete   *island* Greece 39 O12
Crete, Sea of   *sea* Mediterranean Sea
    39 O12
Crimea   *peninsula* Ukraine 39 R6
Croatia   *country* SE Europe 39 L6
Crozet Islands   *island group* French Southern
    & Antarctic Territories 10 E10
Cuba   *country* Caribbean 25 M6
Cuba   *island* Caribbean 11 Q6
Cúcuta   Colombia 27 N2
Cuernavaca   Mexico 24 H7
Cuiabá   Brazil 27 P6
Culiacan   Mexico 24 E5
Curitiba   Brazil 27 Q7
Cusco   Peru 27 N6
Cyclades   *island group* Greece 39 O11
Cyprus   *country* Mediterranean Sea 43 K4
Czech Republic   *country* C Europe 37 O4
Czestochowa   Poland 37 P3

•• D ••

Dakar   *capital city* Senegal 28 F8
Dalalven   *river* Sweden 33 N8
Dalian   China 49 O6
Dallas   Texas, U.S.A. 23 M8
Dalmatia   *cultural region* Croatia 39 L7
Damascus   *capital city* Syria 43 L5
Damavand, Mount   *mountain* Iran 43 P4
Dampier   Western Australia 52 G5
Da Nang   Vietnam 50 J4
Danube   *river* SE Europe 10 D5
Dar es Salaam   Tanzania 31 M6
Darfur   *cultural region* Sudan 29 L9
Darhan   Mongolia 49 L3
Darien, Gulf of   *sea feature* Caribbean
    25 N10
Darling River   *river* Australia 53 N8
Darwin   *territory capital* Northern Territory,
    Australia 53 K2
Dasoguz   Turkmenistan 45 L7
Datong   China 49 M6
Daugavpils   Latvia 33 R10
Davao   Philippines 51 N7
Davis Strait   *sea feature* NW Atlantic Ocean
    58 A6
Dead Sea   *salt lake* Israel/Jordan 43 L5
Debrecen   Hungary 39 N5
Deccan   *plateau* India 47 N7
Delaware   *state* U.S.A. 23 S6
Delhi   India 47 N4
Demchok   *disputed territory* S Asia 47 O2
Denali   *see* McKinley, Mount
Denizli   Turkey 42 J3
Denmark   *country* N Europe 33 L10
Denmark Strait   *sea feature* N Atlantic
    Ocean 58 B7
Denpasar   Indonesia 51 L11
Denver   *state capital* Colorado, U.S.A.
    23 K6

Des Moines *state capital* Iowa, U.S.A. 23 N6
Detroit Michigan, U.S.A. 23 P5
Dhaka *capital city* Bangladesh 47 R5
Dijon France 35 Q7
Dili *capital city* East Timor 51 N11
Divinópolis Brazil 27 R7
Diyarbakir Turkey 43 M3
Djibouti *capital city* Djibouti 29 P9
Djibouti *country* E Africa 29 P9
Dnieper *river* E Europe 10 D4
Dniester *river* Moldova/Ukraine 39 P5
Dnipropetrovs'k Ukraine 39 S5
Dodecanese *island group* Greece 39 P11
Dodoma *capital city* Tanzania 31 M6
Doha *capital city* Qatar 43 P7
Dominica *country* Caribbean 25 S8
Dominican Republic *country* Caribbean 25 P7
Don *river* Russia 40 E7
Donets *river* Ukraine 39 S4
Donets'k Ukraine 39 T5
Dordogne *river* France 35 P8
Dortmund Germany 37 L3
Douala Cameroon 28 J10
Dover *state capital* Delaware, U.S.A. 23 R6
Drakensberg *mountain range* South Africa 31 K11
Drammen Norway 33 M8
Drau or Drava *river* SE Europe 39 L6
Dresden Germany 37 O3
Dubai United Arab Emirates 43 R7
Dublin *capital city* Ireland 35 N4
Dubrovnik Croatia 39 L8
Duero *river* Portugal/Spain 35 M9
Dundee Scotland, U.K. 35 O2
Dunedin New Zealand 56 I11
Durango Mexico 24 F5
Durban South Africa 31 L10
Durres Albania 39 M9
Dushanbe *capital city* Tajikistan 45 O9
Dusseldorf Germany 37 L3
Dzungarian Basin *basin* China 48 H4

• • E • •

East Cape *headland* New Zealand 57 N4
East China Sea *sea* W Pacific Ocean 10 I6
Easter Island *island* Chile 11 O9
Eastern Ghats *mountain range* India 47 O9
East Indies *island group* SE Asia 10 H8
East Siberian Sea *sea* Arctic Ocean 58 D2
East Timor *country* SE Asia 51 O11
Ebro *river* Spain 35 O9
Ecuador *country* W South America 27 M4
Edinburgh *capital city* Scotland, U.K. 35 O3
Edmonton *province capital* Alberta, Canada 20 H8
Efate *island* Vanuatu 55 K8
Egmont, Cape *headland* New Zealand 57 K5
Egypt *country* NE Africa 29 M6
Eindhoven Netherlands 35 Q5
Elbe *river* Czech Republic/Germany 37 N2
El'brus *mountain* Russia 40 D9
El Giza Egypt 29 N6
Ellesmere Island *island* Canada 21 L2
El Paso Texas, U.S.A. 23 K9
El Salvador *country* Central America 24 J9
Empty Quarter *see* Ar Rub' Al Khali
Enderby Land *physical region* Antarctica 59 R7
England *national region* U.K. 35 O4
English Channel *sea feature* NE Atlantic Ocean 35 O5
Equatorial Guinea *country* W Africa 30 G4
Erdenet Mongolia 49 K3
Erebus, Mount *mountain* Antarctica 59 Q11
Erie, Lake *lake* Canada/U.S.A. 23 Q5
Eritrea *country* E Africa 29 O8
Erzurum Turkey 43 M2
Esfahan Iran 43 P5
Eskisehir Turkey 43 K2
Espiritu Santo *island* Vanuatu 55 K8
Espoo Finland 33 Q8
Essen Germany 37 L3
Estonia *country* E Europe 33 Q9
Ethiopia *country* E Africa 29 O10

Ethiopian Highlands *mountain range* Ethiopia 29 O9
Etna, Mount *volcano* Italy 37 O11
Euphrates *river* SW Asia 43 N4
Europe *continent* 10 C4
Everest, Mount *mountain* China/Nepal 47 Q4
Eyre North, Lake *lake* Australia 53 M7

• • F • •

Faeroe Islands *Danish territory* NW Europe 33 K3
Faeroe Islands *island group* NW Europe 10 B3
Faisalabad Pakistan 47 M3
Falkland Islands *U.K. territory* S Atlantic Ocean 27 P11
Falkland Islands *island group* S Atlantic Ocean 11 R11
Farewell, Cape *headland* New Zealand 57 K6
Farg'ona Uzbekistan 45 O8
Faro Portugal 35 L11
Fiji *country* SW Pacific Ocean 55 L9
Fiji *island group* SW Pacific Ocean 11 L8
Finland *country* N Europe 33 Q3
Finland, Gulf of *sea feature* NE Atlantic Ocean 33 Q8
Fiordland *physical region* New Zealand 56 G11
Flinders Range *mountain range* Australia 53 M7
Florence Italy 37 M8
Flores *island* Indonesia 51 M11
Flores Sea *sea* W Pacific Ocean 51 M11
Florianópolis Brazil 27 Q8
Florida *state* U.S.A. 23 Q9
Florida Keys *island group* U.S.A. 23 Q11
Fongafale *capital city* Tuvalu 55 M7
Fortaleza Brazil 27 S4
Fort Worth U.S.A. 23 M8
Foveaux Strait *sea feature* New Zealand 56 H11
France *country* W Europe 35 P7
Frankfort *state capital* Kentucky, U.S.A. 23 P6
Frankfurt am Main Germany 37 M4
Franz Josef Land *island group* Russia 40 J3
Fraser *river* Canada 20 G8
Fredericton *province capital* New Brunswick, Canada 21 P10
Freetown *capital city* Sierra Leone 28 F10
Fremantle Western Australia 52 G9
French Guiana *French territory* N South America 27 Q3
French Polynesia *French territory* C Pacific Ocean 55 Q8
French Southern & Antarctic Territories *French territory* S Indian Ocean 12 F10
Fresno California, U.S.A. 22 G6
Frome, Lake *lake* Australia 53 M8
Fuji, Mt. *mountain* Japan 49 S6
Fukuoka Japan 49 Q7
Funafuti *capital city* Tuvalu 55 M7
Fundy, Bay of *sea feature* Canada 21 P10
Fushun China 49 O5
Futuna *island* Wallis & Futuna 55 M8
Fuzhou China 49 O10

• • G • •

Gabon *country* C Africa 30 H5
Gaborone *capital city* Botswana 31 K9
Gairdner, Lake *lake* Australia 53 L8
Galapagos Islands *island group* Ecuador 27 K4
Galati Romania 39 P7
Galle Sri Lanka 47 O12
Galway Ireland 35 M4
Gambia *country* W Africa 28 E9
Gambier Islands *island group* French Polynesia 55 Q9
Ganges *river* Bangladesh/India 47 Q5
Ganges, Mouths of the *delta* Bangladesh/India 47 R6
Garagum Desert *desert* Turkmenistan 45 L8
Garda, Lake *lake* Italy 37 M6
Gardez Afghanistan 45 O11
Garonne *river* France 35 O8
Gavle Sweden 33 O8

Gaza Strip *disputed territory* SW Asia 43 K5
Gaziantep Turkey 43 L3
Gdansk Poland 37 P1
Geelong Victoria, Australia 53 N11
Geneva Switzerland 37 L6
Geneva, Lake *lake* France/Switzerland 37 K6
Genoa Italy 37 L7
Georgetown *capital city* Guyana 27 P2
George V Land *physical region* Antarctica 59 R11
Georgia *country* SW Asia 43 N2
Georgia *state* U.S.A. 23 Q8
Geraldton Western Australia 52 F8
Germany *country* C Europe 37 M3
Ghaghara *river* India 47 P5
Ghana *country* W Africa 28 H10
Ghaziabad India 47 N4
Ghazni Afghanistan 45 N11
Ghent Belgium 35 Q5
Gibraltar *U.K. territory* SW Europe 35 N12
Gibson Desert *desert* Australia 52 I6
Gijón Spain 35 N8
Gisborne New Zealand 57 N5
Gladstone Queensland, Australia 53 Q6
Glama *river* Norway 33 M8
Glasgow Scotland, U.K. 35 N3
Gobi *desert* China/Mongolia 49 L5
Godavari *river* India 47 O7
Goiânia Brazil 27 Q6
Gold Coast Queensland, Australia 53 Q7
Good Hope, Cape of *headland* South Africa 30 J11
Gothenburg Sweden 33 M9
Gotland *island* Sweden 33 O10
Granada Spain 35 N11
Gran Chaco *plain* C South America 27 O7
Grand Canyon *valley* U.S.A. 22 I7
Grande, Bahía *sea feature* SW Atlantic Ocean 27 O11
Grande, Rio *river* Mexico/U.S.A. 11 P5
Graz Austria 37 O6
Great Australian Bight *sea feature* E Indian Ocean 52 J9
Great Barrier Island *island* New Zealand 57 M3
Great Barrier Reef *reef* Australia 53 P4
Great Basin *basin* U.S.A. 11 O5
Great Bear Lake *lake* Canada 20 H5
Great Dividing Range *mountain range* Australia 53 P9
Greater Antarctica *physical region* Antarctica 59 R9
Greater Antilles *island group* Caribbean 25 L7
Greater Sunda Islands *island group* SE Asia 50 I10
Great Khingan Range *mountain range* China 49 O4
Great Lakes *lakes* Canada/U.S.A. 11 Q4
Great Plain of China *plain* China 10 H5
Great Plains *plain* Canada/U.S.A. 11 O4
Great Rift Valley *valley* Africa/Asia 10 D7
Great Salt Lake *salt lake* U.S.A. 22 I5
Great Sandy Desert *desert* Australia 52 I5
Great Slave Lake *lake* Canada 20 I6
Great Victoria Desert *desert* Australia 52 J7
Great Wall of China *wall* China 49 L6
Greece *country* SE Europe 39 N10
Greenland *Danish territory* NE North America 58 B6
Greenland *island* NE North America 11 S2
Greenland Sea *sea* Arctic Ocean 58 D6
Grenada *country* Caribbean 25 S9
Grenoble France 35 Q8
Greymouth New Zealand 56 J8
Groningen Netherlands 35 Q4
Groznyy Russia 40 E9
Guadalajara Mexico 24 F7
Guadalcanal *island* Solomon Islands 54 J7
Guadalquivir *river* Spain 35 N11
Guadeloupe *French territory* Caribbean 25 S8
Guadiana *river* Spain 35 N10
Guam *U.S. territory* W Pacific Ocean 54 H4
Guangzhou China 49 M11
Guantanamo Bay *U.S. territory* Caribbean 25 O7
Guatemala *country* Central America 24 J8

Guatemala City *capital city* Guatemala 24 J9
Guayaquil Ecuador 27 M4
Guayaquil, Gulf of *sea feature* E Pacific Ocean 27 L4
Guiana Highlands *mountain range* N South America 27 P3
Guinea *country* W Africa 28 F9
Guinea-Bissau *country* W Africa 28 E9
Guinea, Gulf of *sea feature* E Atlantic Ocean 28 I11
Guiyang China 49 L10
Gujranwala Pakistan 47 M3
Gulf, The *sea feature* NW Indian Ocean 43 P6
Gunnbjørn Fjeld *mountain* Greenland 58 C7
Guwahati India 47 R5
Guyana *country* N South America 27 P2
Gyor Hungary 39 M5

• • H • •

Haast New Zealand 56 I9
Hagatna *capital city* Guam 54 I4
Hainan Dao *island* China 49 L12
Hai Phong Vietnam 50 J3
Haiti *country* Caribbean 25 O7
Halifax *province capital* Nova Scotia, Canada 21 Q10
Halmahera *island* Indonesia 51 O9
Hamadan Iran 43 O4
Hamburg Germany 37 M2
Hamersley Range *mountain range* Australia 52 G6
Hamhung North Korea 49 P6
Hamilton Ontario, Canada 21 N11
Hamilton New Zealand 57 L4
Hammerfest Norway 33 P1
Handan China 49 N7
Hangzhou China 49 O9
Ha Noi *capital city* Vietnam 50 I3
Hanover Germany 37 M3
Haora India 47 R6
Harare *capital city* Zimbabwe 31 L8
Harbin China 49 P4
Harrisburg *state capital* Pennsylvania, U.S.A. 23 R6
Hartford *state capital* Connecticut, U.S.A. 23 S5
Hastings New Zealand 57 M6
Hat Yai Thailand 50 H7
Havana *capital city* Cuba 25 L6
Hawaii *state* U.S.A. 22 J11
Hawaii *island* Hawaii, U.S.A. 22 I12
Hawaiian Islands *island group* Hawaii, U.S.A. 55 O2
Heard & McDonald Islands *Australian territory* S Indian Ocean 12 G11
Hefei China 49 N8
Helena *state capital* Montana, U.S.A. 22 I4
Helmand *river* Afghanistan/Iran 45 M12
Helsingborg Sweden 33 M10
Helsinki *capital city* Finland 33 Q8
Herat Afghanistan 45 L10
Hermosillo Mexico 24 E4
Hervey Bay Queensland, Australia 53 Q7
Hiiumaa *island* Estonia 33 P9
Himalayas *mountain range* S Asia 10 G5
Hindu Kush *mountain range* Afghanistan/Pakistan 10 F5
Hiroshima Japan 49 R7
Hispaniola *island* Dominican Republic/Haiti 25 O7
Hkakabo Razi *mountain* Burma/China 50 G1
Hobart *state capital* Tasmania, Australia 53 O12
Ho Chi Minh Vietnam 50 I6
Hodeida Yemen 43 N11
Hohhot China 49 M6
Hokkaido *island* Japan 49 S4
Homs Syria 43 L4
Homyel' Belarus 39 Q3
Honduras *country* Central America 25 K9
Hong Kong China 49 N11
Honiara *capital city* Solomon Islands 54 J7
Honolulu *state capital* Hawaii, U.S.A. 22 I11
Honshu *island* Japan 49 S6
Hormuz, Strait of *sea feature* NW Indian Ocean 43 R7

Nipigon, Lake *lake* Canada **21 L9**
Nis Serbia **39 N8**
Niue *N.Z. territory* S Pacific Ocean **55 N8**
Nizhniy Novgorod Russia **40 F7**
Norfolk Island *Australian territory* SW Pacific Ocean **55 L10**
Norilsk Russia **41 K6**
Norrkoping Sweden **33 N9**
North America *continent* **11 O4**
North Cape *headland* New Zealand **57 K1**
North Cape *headland* Norway **33 P1**
North Carolina *state* U.S.A. **23 R7**
North Dakota *state* U.S.A. **23 L4**
Northern Cook Islands *island group* Cook Islands **55 O8**
Northern Dvina *river* Russia **40 G6**
Northern Ireland *province* U.K. **35 M3**
Northern Mariana Islands *U.S. territory* W Pacific Ocean **54 I3**
Northern Territory *territory* Australia **53 K4**
North European Plain *plain* N Europe **10 D4**
North Island *island* New Zealand **57 M5**
North Korea *country* E Asia **49 P5**
North Pole *pole* Arctic Ocean **58 D4**
North Sea *sea* NE Atlantic Ocean **10 C4**
North Siberian Lowland *lowland* Russia **41 K6**
Northwest Territories *territory* Canada **20 H5**
Norway *country* N Europe **33 M7**
Norwegian Sea *sea* NE Atlantic Ocean **58 D7**
Nouakchott *capital city* Mauritania **28 F8**
Nouméa *capital city* New Caledonia **55 K9**
Nova Scotia *province* Canada **21 Q10**
Nova Scotia *peninsula* Canada **11 R5**
Novaya Zemlya *island group* Russia **40 I5**
Novi Sad Serbia **39 M7**
Novokuznetsk Russia **40 J10**
Novosibirsk Russia **40 J9**
Nowra New South Wales, Australia **53 P10**
Nuku'alofa *capital city* Tonga **55 M9**
Nukus Uzbekistan **45 L7**
Nullarbor Plain *plain* Australia **52 I8**
Nunap Isua *headland* Greenland **58 A7**
Nunavut *territory* Canada **21 K5**
Nuuk *capital city* Greenland **58 A6**
Nyasa, Lake *lake* S Africa **31 M7**
Nyiregyhaza Hungary **39 N5**

• • O • •

Oahu *island* Hawaii, U.S.A. **22 I11**
Oakland California, U.S.A. **22 G6**
Oamaru New Zealand **56 J10**
Oaxaca Mexico **24 H8**
Ob' *river* Russia **40 I7**
Odense Denmark **33 L11**
Oder *river* C Europe **37 O2**
Odesa Ukraine **39 Q6**
Ohio *state* U.S.A. **23 P6**
Ohio *river* U.S.A. **23 P6**
Ohrid, Lake *lake* Albania/Macedonia **39 M9**
Okavango *river* S Africa **30 J8**
Okavango Delta *wetland* Botswana **30 J9**
Okayama Japan **49 R7**
Okeechobee, Lake *lake* U.S.A. **23 R10**
Okhotsk, Sea of *sea* NW Pacific Ocean **41 Q8**
Oklahoma *state* U.S.A. **23 M8**
Oklahoma City *state capital* Oklahoma, U.S.A. **23 M7**
Oland *island* Sweden **33 O10**
Olduvai Gorge *valley* Tanzania **31 M5**
Olympia *state capital* Washington, U.S.A. **22 H3**
Omaha Nebraska, U.S.A. **23 M6**
Oman *country* SW Asia **43 R9**
Oman, Gulf of *sea feature* NW Indian Ocean **43 R7**
Omdurman Sudan **29 N8**
Omsk Russia **40 I9**
Onega, Lake *lake* Russia **40 F6**
Ontario *province* Canada **21 L8**
Ontario, Lake *lake* Canada/U.S.A. **23 R4**
Oporto Portugal **35 L9**
Oran Algeria **28 I4**
Orange River *river* S Africa **30 J10**
Orebro *town* Sweden **33 N9**

Oregon *state* U.S.A. **22 H4**
Orenburg Russia **40 G9**
Oreor *capital city* Palau **54 H5**
Orinoco *river* Colombia/Venezuela **27 O2**
Orkney Islands *island group* Scotland, U.K. **35 O1**
Orlando Florida, U.S.A. **23 Q9**
Orléans France **35 P6**
Orumiyeh Iran **43 N3**
Oruro Bolivia **27 O6**
Osaka Japan **49 R7**
Osh Kyrgyzstan **45 P8**
Oshawa Ontario, Canada **21 N11**
Osijek Croatia **39 M6**
Oslo *capital city* Norway **33 M8**
Ostersund Sweden **33 N6**
Ostrava Czech Republic **37 P4**
Ottawa *capital city* Ontario, Canada **21 O10**
Ouagadougou *capital city* Burkina Faso **28 H9**
Oulu Finland **33 Q5**
Ounasjoki *river* Finland **33 Q4**
Outer Hebrides *island group* Scotland, U.K. **35 M1**
Oviedo Spain **35 M8**

• • P • •

Pacific Ocean *ocean* **11 L5**
Padang Indonesia **50 H9**
Pago Pago *capital city* American Samoa **55 N8**
Pakistan *country* S Asia **47 K3**
Pakxé Laos **50 I5**
Palau *country* W Pacific Ocean **54 G5**
Palawan *island* Philippines **51 L6**
Palembang Indonesia **50 I10**
Palermo Italy **37 N11**
Palikir *capital city* Micronesia **54 J5**
Palk Strait *sea feature* N Indian Ocean **47 O10**
Palliser, Cape *headland* New Zealand **57 L7**
Palma Spain **35 P10**
Palmyra Atoll *U.S. territory* C Pacific Ocean **55 O5**
Palu Indonesia **51 M9**
Pamir *river* Afghanistan/Tajikistan **45 P9**
Pamirs *mountain range* C Asia **45 P9**
Pampas *plain* Argentina **27 O9**
Panama *country* Central America **25 M11**
Panama Canal *canal* Panama **25 M10**
Panama City *capital city* Panama **25 M10**
Panay *island* Philippines **51 M6**
Papeete *capital city* French Polynesia **55 Q8**
Papua *province* Indonesia **51 R10**
Papua New Guinea *country* SW Pacific Ocean **54 I6**
Paracel Islands *disputed territory* SE Asia **12 H6**
Paraguay *country* C South America **27 P7**
Paraguay *river* C South America **11 R9**
Paramaribo *capital city* Suriname **27 Q2**
Paraná *river* C South America **27 P8**
Paris *capital city* France **35 P6**
Patagonia *physical region* Argentina/Chile **27 O11**
Patna India **47 Q5**
Patos, Lagoa dos *sea feature* SW Atlantic Ocean **27 Q8**
Patra Greece **39 N10**
Pavlodar Kazakhstan **45 P3**
Peace *river* Canada **20 I7**
Pechora *river* Russia **40 H6**
Pecs Hungary **39 M6**
Pegu Burma **50 G4**
Peipus, Lake *lake* Estonia **33 Q9**
Pekanbaru Indonesia **50 H9**
Peloponnese *peninsula* Greece **39 N11**
Pennsylvania *state* U.S.A. **23 Q5**
Penza Russia **40 F8**
Perm' Russia **40 G8**
Perpignan France **35 P9**
Perth *state capital* Western Australia **52 G9**
Peru *country* W South America **27 M5**
Peshawar Pakistan **47 L2**
Peter I Island *Norwegian territory* Southern Ocean **59 N9**
Petra *archaeological site* Jordan **43 L6**

Petropavlovsk Kazakhstan **45 O2**
Petropavlovsk-Kamchatskiy Russia **41 R8**
Petrozavodsk Russia **40 F6**
Philadelphia *town* Pennsylvania, U.S.A. **23 R5**
Philippine Islands *island group* SE Asia **10 I7**
Philippines *country* SE Asia **51 M6**
Philippine Sea *sea* W Pacific Ocean **10 I6**
Phnom Penh *capital city* Cambodia **50 I6**
Phoenix *state capital* Arizona, U.S.A. **22 I8**
Phoenix Islands *island group* Kiribati **55 M7**
Phuket *island* Thailand **50 G7**
Pierre *state capital* South Dakota, U.S.A. **23 L5**
Pinar del Rio Cuba **25 L6**
Pindos Mountains *mountain range* Greece **39 N10**
Piraeus Greece **39 O10**
Pitcairn Islands *U.K. territory* C Pacific Ocean **55 R9**
Pitcairn Islands *island group* S Pacific Ocean **11 N9**
Pittsburgh Pennsylvania, U.S.A. **23 Q6**
Piura Peru **27 M4**
Plata, Río de la *sea feature* SW Atlantic Ocean **27 P9**
Plenty, Bay of *sea feature* New Zealand **57 M4**
Ploiesti Romania **39 P7**
Plovdiv Bulgaria **39 O8**
Plymouth England, U.K. **35 N5**
Plzen Czech Republic **37 N4**
Po *river* Italy **37 M7**
Pobedy, Pik *mountain* China/Kyrgyzstan **45 R7**
Podgorica *capital city* Montenegro **39 M8**
Pohnpei *island* Micronesia **54 J5**
Pokhara Nepal **47 P4**
Poland *country* C Europe **37 P3**
Poltava Ukraine **39 R4**
Polynesia *island group* C Pacific Ocean **55 N7**
Pontianak Indonesia **50 J9**
Port-au-Prince *capital city* Haiti **25 O7**
Port Elizabeth South Africa **31 K11**
Port Hedland Western Australia **52 G5**
Portland Oregon, U.S.A. **22 H4**
Port Louis *capital city* Mauritius **31 P9**
Port Macquarie New South Wales, Australia **53 Q8**
Port Moresby *capital city* Papua New Guinea **54 I7**
Porto Alegre Brazil **27 Q8**
Porto-Novo *capital city* Benin **28 I10**
Porto Velho Brazil **27 O5**
Port Sudan Sudan **29 O7**
Portugal *country* SW Europe **35 M10**
Port-Vila *capital city* Vanuatu **55 K8**
Potosí Bolivia **27 O7**
Po Valley *valley* Italy **37 M7**
Poznan Poland **37 P3**
Prague *capital city* Czech Republic **37 O4**
Praia *capital city* Cape Verde **28 E8**
Prespa, Lake *lake* SE Europe **39 N9**
Pretoria *see* Tshwane
Prince Edward Island *province* Canada **21 Q9**
Prince Edward Islands *island group* South Africa **10 D10**
Prince George British Columbia, Canada **20 G8**
Pripet *river* Belarus/Ukraine **39 P3**
Pripet Marshes *wetland* Belarus/Ukraine **39 O3**
Pristina *capital city* Kosovo **39 N8**
Prome Burma **50 G4**
Providence *state capital* Rhode Island, U.S.A. **23 S5**
Prudhoe Bay Alaska, U.S.A. **22 G9**
Prut *river* SE Europe **39 P6**
Puebla Mexico **24 H7**
Puerto Ayacucho Venezuela **27 O2**
Puerto Montt Chile **27 N10**
Puerto Rico *U.S. territory* Caribbean **25 Q7**
Puncak Jaya *mountain* Indonesia **51 R10**
Pune India **47 M7**
Punta Arenas Chile **27 O12**
Purus *river* Brazil/Peru **27 O4**
Pusan South Korea **49 Q7**

Putumayo *river* N South America **27 N4**
P'yongyang *capital city* North Korea **49 P6**
Pyrenees *mountain range* SW Europe **35 P9**

• • Q • •

Qaanaaq Greenland **58 B5**
Qaidam Basin *basin* China **48 I6**
Qaqortoq Greenland **58 A7**
Qarshi Uzbekistan **45 N8**
Qatar *country* SW Asia **43 P7**
Qilian Shan *mountain range* China **48 I6**
Qingdao China **49 O7**
Qiqihar China **49 O4**
Qom Iran **43 P4**
Québec *province capital* Québec, Canada **21 O10**
Québec *province* Canada **21 O8**
Queen Charlotte Islands *island group* Canada **20 F7**
Queen Elizabeth Islands *island group* Canada **20 J3**
Queen Maud Land *physical region* Antarctica **59 Q7**
Queen Maud Mountains *mountain range* Antarctica **59 P9**
Queensland *state* Australia **53 N5**
Queenstown New Zealand **56 H10**
Queretaro Mexico **24 G7**
Quetta Pakistan **47 K3**
Quito *capital city* Ecuador **27 M4**

• • R • •

Rabat *capital city* Morocco **28 H5**
Rach Gia Vietnam **50 I6**
Rajkot India **47 L6**
Rajshahi Bangladesh **47 R5**
Raleigh *state capital* North Carolina, U.S.A. **23 R7**
Ralik Chain *island group* Marshall Islands **55 K5**
Ranchi India **47 Q6**
Rangitikei *river* New Zealand **57 M6**
Rarotonga *island* Cook Islands **55 O9**
Rasht Iran **43 P3**
Ratak Chain *island group* Marshall Islands **55 L4**
Rawalpindi Pakistan **47 M2**
Recife Brazil **27 T5**
Red Deer Alberta, Canada **20 H8**
Red River *river* U.S.A. **23 M8**
Red Sea *sea* NW Indian Ocean **10 D6**
Regina *province capital* Saskatchewan, Canada **20 J9**
Reims France **35 Q6**
Reindeer Lake *lake* Canada **20 J7**
Rennes France **35 O6**
Réunion *French territory* SW Indian Ocean **31 O9**
Réunion *island* W Indian Ocean **10 E9**
Revillagigedo, Islas *island group* Mexico **24 D7**
Reykjavik *capital city* Iceland **33 L2**
Rhine *river* W Europe **10 C4**
Rhode Island *state* U.S.A. **23 S5**
Rhodes *island* Greece **39 Q11**
Rhodope Mountains *mountain range* Bulgaria **39 N8**
Rhône *river* France/Switzerland **35 Q8**
Richmond *state capital* Virginia, U.S.A. **23 R6**
Riga *capital city* Latvia **33 Q10**
Riga, Gulf of *sea feature* NE Atlantic Ocean **33 Q9**
Rijeka Croatia **39 K6**
Rio Branco Brazil **27 O5**
Rio de Janeiro Brazil **27 R7**
Riyadh *capital city* Saudi Arabia **43 O8**
Rockhampton Queensland, Australia **53 Q6**
Rocky Mountains *mountain range* Canada/U.S.A. **11 O4**
Romania *country* SE Europe **39 O6**
Rome *capital city* Italy **37 N9**
Ronne Ice Shelf *ice shelf* Antarctica **59 O8**
Rosario Argentina **27 P9**
Ross Ice Shelf *ice shelf* Antarctica **59 P10**
Ross Sea *sea* Southern Ocean **59 P11**
Rostov-na-Donu Russia **40 D8**
Rotorua New Zealand **57 M4**
Rotorua, Lake *lake* New Zealand **57 M4**

General index

Picture sources

Picthall and Gunzi would like to thank the following individuals and organizations for their permission to use their photographs:

Abbreviations
t = top; b = bottom; c = center;
r = right; l = left.

Aloysius Han - www.geohavens.com for the rubies on p50; Alstom; Automobili Lamborghini SpA; CN Tower, Canada; Dickinson by Design; Ford Motor Company; International Crane Foundation, Baraboo, Wisconsin; Jumeirah International; Memories of New Zealand - www.memoriesofnz.co.nz; Saab Great Britain Ltd

Ardea: John Wombe/Auscape/Ardea.com 53 bc

Britain on View: www.britainonview.com 34 bc

Bruce Coleman: 55 cr

Corbis: Tiziana and Gianni Baldizzone: 32 tr; Sharna Balfour; Gallo Images: 31 tr; Tom Bean: 36 bl; Fernando Bengoechea/Beateworks: 35 tr; Tibor Bognar: 46 cl, 46 cl; Christophe Boisvieux: 17 br; Simonpietri Christian/Corbis Sygma: 9 br; Arko Datta/Reuters: 46 cl; Colin Dixon/Arcaid: 38 crb; DLILLC: 30 bc, 56 cr; epa: 14 cl; Alejandro Ernesto/epa: 14 bl; Randy Faris: 24 bl; Paddy Fields -

Louie Psihoyos: 50 bl; Franz Marc Frei: 56 bl; Natalie Fobes: 35 br; Owen Franken: 17 tr; Darrell Gulin: 15 tr; Ainal Abd Halim/Reuters: 42 tr; Lindsay Hebberd: 17 tl; Chris Hellier: 31 cr; Dallas and John Heaton/ Free Agents Limited: 29 br, 49 tr; Jon Hicks: 27 br; Robert van der Hilst: 38 cl; Eric and David Hosking: 15 bcl; Hanan Isachar: 43 tr; Wolfgang Kaehler: 15 tl,15 br, 54 bl; Catherine Karnow: 38 cr, 55 tr; Frank Krahmer/zefa: 27 cl; Jacques Langevin/Corbis Sygma: 41 tr; Danny Lehman: 25 br; John and Lisa Merrill: 36 c; Viviane Moos: 46 tr; Kazuyoshi Nomachi: 29 tc; Neil Rabinowitz: 57 cr; Finbarr O'Reilly/Reuters: 16 tr; José Fuste Raga/zefa: 14 br, 22 bl, 34 cr, 49 br, 50 c; Carmen Redondo: 32 br; Reuters: 26 cr, 53 tr; Guenter Rossenbach/zefa: 15 tcl; Galen Rowell: 55 tl, 58 cr; Anders Ryman: 52 cl; Kevin Schafer: 9 bc; Alfio Scigliano/Sygma/Corbis: 37 br; Paul Seheult/Eye Ubiquitous: 26 tr, Hugh Sitton/zefa: 51 tl; Hubert Stadler: 15 tcr; Paul A. Souders: 33 cr; Jon Sparks: 42 bl; Shannon Stapleton/Reuters: 16 bl; Hans Strand: 56 tr; Staffan Widstrand: 37 cr; Uli Wiesmeier/zefa: 36 tr; Tony Wharton/Frank Lane Picture Agency: 37 br; Larry Williams: 25 tr; Valdrin Xhemaj/epa: 21 tc; Shamil Zhumatov/Reuters: 44 c.

ESA: 8 cl, c, cr, 9 cl, c, ca, cr.

FLPA: Ingo Arndt/Foto NaturaI/Minden Pictures: 38 bc; Richard Becker: 14 tr; Jim Brandenburg/Minden Pictures: 48 cl; Hans Dieter Brandl: 32 cr; Michael Callan: 32 cl; R.Dirscherl: 51 cr;

Gerry Ellis/Minden Pictures: 48 bl; im Fitzharris/Minden Pictures/FLPA: 20 bl; Michael & Patricia Fogden/Minden Pictures: 24 bc; Michael Gore: 52 c; Rev. Bruce Henry: 46 br; Michio Hoshino/Minden Pictures: 23 tr, 58 br; Mitsuaki Iwago /Minden Pictures: 52 bc; Frank W Lane: 45 tr; Frans Lanting: 23 bc, 26 bc, 29 cr; Thomas Mangelsen/Minden Picture: 4-5 b; S & D & K Maslowski: 20 bc; Claus Meyer/Minden Pictures: 26 cl; Yva Momatiuk /John Eastcott/Minden Pictures: 27 tr; Colin Monteath /Minden Pictures: 47 tr; Rinie van Muers/Foto Natura: 3 c, 59 tr; Mark Newman: 41 tl; Flip Nicklin/Minden Picture: 21 tr; R & M Van Nostrand: 28 bl; Alan Parker: 44 bl; Walter Rohdich: 46 cr; L Lee Rue: 21 cr; Cyril Ruoso\JH Editorial/Minden Pictures: 36 br; Silvestris Fotoservice: 39 cr; Jurgen & Christine Sohns: 31 tc, 44 br; Inga Spence: 42 bc; Egmont Strigl/ Imagebroker/FLPA: 45 br; Chris & Tilde Stuart: 43 br; Terry Andrewartha: 58 tr; Barbara Todd/ Hedgehog House/Minden Pictures: 59 cr; Winfried Wisniewski: 40 cl, 59 bl; Terry Whittaker: 34 tr; Konrad Wothe/Minden Pictures: 40 bc; Zhinong Xi/Minden Pictures: 49 tl; Shin Yoshino/Minden Pictures: 53 cr.

Andy Crawford: 51 br

Steve Gorton: 24 c, 34 cl, 36 c, 38 tc, bc, 41 bl, 42 c, 45 tl, cr, 47 cl, bc, 49 cr, 51 c, 54 tr, 54 tr, 54 bc

NASA: 9 tr, 23 br.

Chez Picthall: 2 b, 23 tc, 41 br.

Peter Picthall: 28 cl

Still Pictures: K. Thomas/Still Pictures: 39 tl

Warren Photographic: Jane Burton: 39 br, 50 tr, 57 br; Kim Taylor and Mark Taylor: 32 c; Mark Taylor: 50 tl, Monarch butterflies © Warren Photographic: 24 tc.

Dominic Zwemmer: 14 cl, 15 bc, 30 cl, 53 br, 57 ac

Front cover
Main image: NASA; Tim Graham/Corbis: tl; DLILLC/Corbis: cl; Michael Gore FLPA: clb; Cyril Ruoso\JH Editoria/Minden Pictures/FLPA: bl.

Back cover
Jose Fuste Raga/Corbis: tl, cl; Warren photographic: clb; NASA: bl.

All other images © of Picthall and Gunzi.

Every effort has been made to trace the copyright holders and we apologise in advance for any unintentional omissions. We would be pleased to insert the appropriate acknowledgement in any subsequent edition of this book.

Continents of the world

ATLANTIC
OCEAN

EUROPE

ASIA

AFRICA

ATLANTIC
OCEAN

INDIAN
OCEAN

AUST

SOUTHERN OCEAN